The Jihadist Plot

THE UNTOLD STORY OF AL-QAEDA
AND THE LIBYAN REBELLION

John Rosenthal

ENCOUNTER DIGITAL

The Jihadist Plot: The Untold Story of Al-Qaeda and the Libyan Rebellion was first published as an ebook as part of the Encounter Digital imprint.

© 2013 by John Rosenthal

First American edition published in 2013 by Encounter Books, an activity of Encounter for Culture and Education, Inc., a nonprofit, tax exempt corporation.
Encounter Books website address: www.encounterbooks.com

Manufactured in the United States and printed on acid-free paper. The paper used in this publication meets the minimum requirements of ANSI/NISO Z39.48–1992 (R 1997) (*Permanence of Paper*).

FIRST AMERICAN EDITION

LIBRARY OF CONGRESS CATALOGING-IN-PUBLICATION DATA
Rosenthal, John, 1961–
The Jihadist plot: the untold story of al-Qaeda and the Libyan rebellion/ John Rosenthal.
pages cm
Includes bibliographical references and index.
ISBN 978-1-59403-717-7 (pbk.: alk. paper)—ISBN 978-1-59403-682-8 (ebook)
1. Libya—History—Civil War, 2011– 2. Qaida (Organization) I. Title.
DT236.R58 2013
961.204'2—dc23

2013005201

CONTENTS

CONTENTS

PREFACE

"How could this happen? How could this happen in a country we helped liberate, in a city we helped save from destruction?" Thus Secretary of State Hillary Clinton expressed what she supposed was the reaction of many Americans to the September 11, 2012 attacks in Benghazi that left American ambassador to Libya Chris Stevens and three other Americans dead. The questioning and self-doubt showed "just how confounding the world can be," Clinton observed. But the world is not so confounding when one is correctly informed, and the Benghazi attacks are not so confusing and "senseless" as the Obama administration insists. They are in fact the direct consequence of American policy in supporting the Libyan rebellion against Muammar al-Qaddafi, and they make perfect sense when one knows how thoroughly the rebel forces were affiliated with and inspired by al-Qaeda.

Those same forces proudly fly the al-Qaeda flag to this day. They do so not in secretive "jihadi encampments"—such as those for which drones dispatched by the Obama administration are reportedly searching in Eastern Libya. They do so rather in broad daylight on the main boulevards of Benghazi and other Libyan cities. One does not need drones or sophisticated surveillance technology to find them. Videos of the military parades of the Libyan *mujahideen*—to use their own preferred terminology—are readily available on local Arabic-language websites and YouTube pages.

These are not "small groups" of extremists, as Hillary Clinton assured the American public on the day after the Benghazi attacks. They are the very rebel brigades that formed the military backbone of the rebellion on the ground and that were able to push forward to victory thanks only to the massive air support that they received from America and its NATO allies. As will be seen in the pages to follow, the rebel military commanders on virtually all the major fronts of the Libyan war were al-Qaeda-linked radicals. The rebel brigades have not disbanded; they have not laid down their weapons; and, for all intents and purposes, it is they who dictate their law to the nominal Libyan government and not vice-versa—or rather it is they who, per their own ideology, uphold the law of Allah against all deviations and "foreign machinations."

Indeed, as will likewise be seen in the following pages, even the brigade that is reported to have provided an escort for marines sent to evacuate personnel from the American consulate on the night of the Benghazi attack is known to fly the black flags of al-Qaeda. This perhaps helps to explain why the supposedly secret "safe house" in which consulate personnel took refuge turned out to be neither secret nor safe, but was the target of a second attack.

Attacks on Western consulates are nothing new in Benghazi. The anti-Qaddafi rebellion is officially known as the February 17th Revolution, in honor of the February 17, 2011 protests that sparked the uprising. But how many Americans know that those protests were timed to commemorate an earlier assault on a Western consulate? On February 17, 2006, the Italian consulate in Benghazi was besieged and set ablaze by a mob of thousands, who had been whipped into a frenzy by Islamist media and Friday prayers following an Italian politician's defense of the famous "Mohammed cartoons." The Italian consulate personnel managed to escape harm, because the Libyan security forces of the time stood their ground and protected them. According to eyewitness reports, the members of the Libyan security detachment at the U.S. consulate on the night of September 11, 2012 quickly fled their posts.

Moreover, something else significant had changed in the meanwhile. The mob that stormed the Italian consulate in 2006 was extremely violent, but it was unarmed. It was really just a mob. On September 11, 2012, the American consulate and its "safe house" were attacked by an apparently well-trained armed force using heavy artillery and RPGs.

This too is a direct result of American and allied policy. Under the approving eye of the Western world—or, at any rate, of Western governments—Libya's Islamist rebels were not only permitted to raid the military stores of the old regime, but they were also armed and trained by sympathetic Gulf monarchies. Indeed, at least one Western nation—France—has admitted to providing arms to the rebels itself. One can see the Libyan *mujahideen* parading their military wares—mortars, heavy machine-guns, shoulder-fired grenade launchers—in some of the videos mentioned above.

Tens of thousands of Libyans have died as a consequence of the NATO intervention in Libya: whether victims of NATO bombing or of the horrific atrocities committed by the rebels, whether ardent supporters of the old regime or merely people who preferred it to the severe and intolerant form of Islam embraced by the rebellion. Now, four Americans have died as a consequence of NATO's Libya adventure as well. There is reason to believe they will not be the last.

—John Rosenthal
September 20, 2012

POSTSCRIPT

Since I wrote the above lines, it has become clear that the primary target of the 9/11 Benghazi attacks was not in fact a consulate—even if much of the media, in keeping with the initial reports, continues to describe it as such. It was rather a small US diplomatic mission devoted to maintaining and cultivating contacts in the Eastern Libyan cradle of the anti-Qaddafi rebellion.

Moreover, thanks to the release of unclassified diplomatic cables by the House Oversight Committee, we now know that only two days before the attacks American officials in Benghazi met with one of the jihadist protagonists of this book: Wisam bin Hamid, a reputed veteran of jihad in Afghanistan and Iraq and the commander of Libya Shield, the most powerful Islamist brigade in Eastern Libya. It was Libya Shield that allegedly came to the aid of American marines on the night of the attacks. But, as will be seen in the following pages, Libya Shield does not only fly the same black flags as Ansar al-Sharia, the allegedly al-Qaeda-linked militia that has been widely accused of perpetrating the attacks. It also shares exactly the same program and ideology.

CHAPTER 1

Introduction: Changing Sides in the War on Terror

Once upon a time, there was a "war on terror." The term was highly contested, because it focused on a tactic and left unspecified the practitioners of that tactic with whom the United States and some relatively few allies were at war for the greater part of the first decade of the 21st century. The war on terror was in fact, more precisely, a war on al-Qaeda and affiliated Islamic terror groups, which share al-Qaeda's ideology and methods. But for all its problems, at least the term had the advantage of making clear that the US and its allies abhorred the tactic in question.

They do not anymore. A remarkable development took place in the midst of the 2011 conflict in Libya: the United States and its allies changed sides in the war on terror. From virtually the very start of the unrest in Libya in mid-February 2011, there were troubling signs that the insurgents, whom the Western media insisted on presenting as peaceful "protestors," were in fact violent Islamic extremists whose methods bore a clear resemblance to those of al-Qaeda. Indeed, the methods of the rebels—including beheadings and summary group executions by shots to the back of the head—clearly resembled not merely those of al-Qaeda, but of that branch of al-Qaeda that was most notorious for its brutality: namely, Abu Musab al-Zarqawi's al-Qaeda in Iraq.

The resemblance, as it turns out, was not accidental. Famous for its religious fanaticism, the eastern Libyan heartland of the Libyan rebellion was in fact well-known in counter-terrorism circles as a hotbed of support for al-Zarqawi's al-Qaeda in Iraq. Within weeks of the outbreak of the rebellion, moreover, a leading rebel commander—probably *the* leading rebel commander of the first phase of the rebellion—was openly admitting his al-Qaeda ties to European journalists and casually noting that his troops included veterans of al-Qaeda's Iraqi jihad. This is to say that by mid-March 2011 some of the same forces that only a few years earlier were executing and mutilating American servicemen and civilians in Iraq were now reaping the benefit of crushing American air support in their jihad against Muammar al-Qaddafi in Libya.

Like all the signs of the rebels' radical Islamic inspiration and terrorist methods, such admissions were simply ignored by the traditional American media. Indeed, as will be seen in chapter 6, the very same rebel commander could even appear in the pages of America's supposed newspaper of record as a picture of Islamic moderation.

Some five months later, massive NATO bombing of Tripoli would bring about the collapse of the *ancien régime*, allowing the rebels to walk in and seize control of the Libyan capital. It was only then that the traditional news media could no longer shield their eyes—and those of their publics—from the leading role being played by Islamic radicals in the anti-Qaddafi rebellion. The new military governor of rebel-controlled Tripoli was, after all, none other than the historical leader of Libya's own al-Qaeda affiliate, the Libyan Islamic Fighting Group (LIFG). To sweeten the pill, the news media engaged in a furious process of historical revisionism: virtually overnight they transformed the hitherto notorious Libyan terror group into a patriotic organization that was merely dedicated—just like America and its allies—to freeing Libya from tyranny.

Two months after that, NATO airstrikes would drive Muammar al-Qaddafi into the hands of the rebel forces that abused and murdered him outside of Sirte. Thereupon, the internationally-recognized political chief of the rebellion, National Transitional Council Chair Mustapha Abdul Jalil, announced the official "liberation" of Libya—and, at the same time, the immediate abrogation of all Libyan laws that conflict with the *sharia*. Merely days after that, the black flag of al-Qaeda was spotted flying over the courthouse in Benghazi, the original headquarters and symbolic cradle of the Libyan rebellion.

The flag-sighting was largely dismissed in the West as an aberration. But, ever so briefly, some Western commentators now ventured to express hesitant concerns about the role that Islamic extremism might play in post-Qaddafi Libya. The prospect of fundamentalists gaining the upper-hand was depicted as an unintended consequence of a democratic uprising—a matter of Islamists rushing to fill the "vacuum" left by the toppling of the tyrant.

But there was no vacuum to be filled. The streets of Benghazi were in fact awash with al-Qaeda flags in the days following Libya's "liberation." As will be seen in chapter 3, they have been raised in Benghazi and elsewhere in post-Qaddafi Libya by the very forces with which NATO partnered to bring about the demise of Qaddafi and his Arab Socialist *Jamahiriya* or "state of the masses."

There is nothing surprising about this. Pace the mythology created by Western governments and Western media, the Libyan uprising was not the product of the spontaneous democratic aspirations of the Libyan people. It was the product rather of the aspirations of al-Qaeda-linked Islamic extremists who had long been plotting to overturn Qaddafi's "apostate" regime by using precisely the terrorist methods that would be brought to bear against it in February 2011.

The existence and contours of this plot will be documented in chapter 9. As will likewise be shown, moreover, the Libyan Islamists' longstanding obsession with their "near enemy," Muammar al-Qaddafi, by no means prevented them not only from fighting against America and its allies on the frontlines of jihad in Iraq and Afghanistan, but also from contributing to al-Qaeda's grand strategy of striking America and its allies at home in the West.

The Jihadist Plot tells the real story of the Libyan rebellion and the Islamic extremists who made it: men like Abdul-Hakim al-Hasadi, the most prominent commander of the rebellion on the Eastern front; Abdul-Hakim Belhadj, the supreme military commander of the Libyan Islamic Fighting Group; Abu al-Munthir al-Saadi, the LIFG's chief religious authority and strategist; and the hitherto little known Wisam bin Hamid, the youthful rebel field commander who directed the siege of Sirte from the ground while NATO forces pounded Qaddafi's last refuge from the air.

A NOTE ON SOURCES AND TRANSLATIONS

While it was still being seriously pursued, the war on terror left behind traces in the form of court records from terror trials in the United States and allied countries, published United Nations and US government decisions proscribing terror suspects, and classified State Department and Department of Defense reports, many of which have since been leaked. The evidence assembled here is drawn largely from such residual traces of the war on terror, crucially including Spanish, Italian and British court records and police reports.

The evidence also crucially includes video and text from local pro-rebellion Libyan sources and Islamist websites. These Arabic sources provide the most striking confirmation of the religious fervor that was the driving force of the rebellion. They have hitherto gone virtually entirely ignored in the West. All links to the video evidence cited here were working at the time the book went to press. There is, of course, no guarantee that the videos will continue to be available online at the given URLs or at all. The author is in possession of copies of the clips in question.

All translations from French, German, Italian, Spanish and Dutch are by the author. Where another source is not given, translations from Arabic are by Maureen Millington-Brodie. Ms. Millington-Brodie's contributions are especially important in chapters 3 and 6.

CHAPTER 2

The Mohammed Cartoons and the Eastern Libyan Uprising

The Libyan rebellion is officially known as the "February 17 revolution" in honor of February 17, 2011: the scheduled date of protests in Benghazi that are widely credited with having sparked the anti-Qaddafi uprising. In fact, the mere announcement of the "Day of Rage," as organizers dubbed it, had provoked counter-measures by the Libyan regime, and, spurred on by events in neighboring Egypt, protests—as well as violent clashes with Libyan security forces—had already begun earlier.

But the date of February 17 was not chosen at random. The 2011 Benghazi protests commemorated protests that occurred in Benghazi five years earlier on February 17, 2006. The target of the 2006 protests was none other than the "Mohammed cartoons," the Islamist source of outrage *par excellence*.

The February 17 protests in 2006 would lead to the storming of the Italian consulate in Benghazi by an angry mob. Two days earlier, then Italian Reforms Minister Roberto Calderoli had appeared on Italy's *RAI Uno* public television wearing a t-shirt with a cartoon of

Mohammed printed on it. As Calderoli explained, the gesture was meant as a statement in favor of freedom of expression.

Calderoli's intentions were also clear from the cartoon he chose for the t-shirt. It was not one of the famous twelve cartoons from the Danish newspaper *Jyllands-Posten* that first sparked the so-called Mohammed cartoon controversy. Rather, it was a cartoon that was published on the front page of the February 1 edition of the French newspaper *France Soir* and that represented an obvious commentary on the controversy. The *France Soir* cartoon shows Mohammed in heaven in the company of other religious figures, one of whom—apparently Jesus—tells him, "Don't grumble, Mohammed, all of us here have been caricatured." The edition of *France Soir* likewise reprinted the *Jyllands-Posten* cartoons on inside pages. On the very day of its appearance, *France Soir* editor-in-chief Jacques Lefranc was fired by the CEO of the paper, who offered his apologies for the publication of the cartoons.

Not all publishers were so squeamish, however. On the same day, February 1, several other European papers, including Germany's *Die Welt* and Italy's *La Stampa*, likewise reprinted some or all of the *Jyllands-Posten* cartoons, and they did so unapologetically. In the following days, still more papers followed suit, some of them citing Lefranc's sacking as having provided the impulse for their decision. "We're not doing it as a provocation," Peter Vandermeersch, the editor in chief of the Flemish daily *De Standaard* explained, "But our press freedom is in danger and we have to be able to react."

The reprints added fuel to the fire of a controversy that—after appearing to have nearly died out around the New Year—was being energetically stoked by Muslim activists. Chief among the latter was the Qatari-based Islamic cleric Yusuf al-Qaradawi. An Egyptian by birth, al-Qaradawi went into exile in the 1970s, fleeing the Egyptian government's repression of the Muslim Brotherhood. Although he holds no formal position within the Brotherhood, al-Qaradawi is widely recognized as the "spiritual leader" of the organization. He is reported to have turned down the formal leadership of the Brother-hood's Egyptian "mothership" on several occasions, most recently in 2004.

On January 21, 2006, in his capacity as president of the International Union of Muslim Scholars (IUMS), al-Qaradawi issued a statement calling on Denmark and Norway to take a "firm stand" against the "insults to the Prophet" represented by the cartoons and threatening a Muslim boycott of Danish and Norwegian products if this failed to happen. The small Norwegian newspaper *Magazinet* had already reprinted the Danish cartoons earlier in the month. Remarks by the Danish prime minister defending freedom of expression were cited in the IUMS statement as further "injur[ing] the feelings of millions of Muslims around the world."[1]

Two weeks later, following the reprinting of the cartoons in *Le Soir* and other European papers, al-Qaradawi upped the ante, moving from economic threats to threats of a different order. In a new statement issued by the IUMS on February 2, al-Qaradawi called on Muslims to make the following day, a Friday, an international "day of rage" against the cartoons. In his own Friday sermon on February 3, al-Qaradawi set the tone. "The *ummah* [the Islamic community] must rage in anger," he urged,

> It is told that Imam al-Shafi'i said: "Whoever was angered and did not rage is a jackass." We are not an *ummah* of jackasses. We are not jackasses for riding, but lions that roar. We are lions that zealously protect their dens, and avenge affronts to their sanctities. We

---

1. IUMS statement signed by IUMS President Yusuf al-Qaradawi and IUMS Secretary General Mohammad Salim Al-Awa. According to a report published the same day by IslamOnline.net, the statement was originally issued on January 21, 2006. The Muslim-themed website was founded by Qaradawi and served at the time as one of the principal platforms for his edicts and exhortations. A widely available English translation of the IUMS statement is dated January 29, 2006.

are not an *ummah* of jackasses. We are an *ummah* that should rage
for the sake of Allah, His Prophet, and His Book.[2]

Al-Qaradawi's call for "rage" was broadcast by the Qatari-based
satellite channel Al Jazeera. As the host of a popular weekly program
on "Sharia and Life," Al-Qaradawi has long been a fixture on the
channel. Previously best known in the West as the principal conduit
for the video messages of Osama bin Laden and al-Qaeda, Al Jazeera
would now serve as the most powerful bullhorn at al-Qaradawi's
disposal, assuring that the "cartoon jihad" he had unleashed would
resonate throughout the Arab-speaking world.

On the appointed Friday, February 3, Al-Jazeera dedicated extensive programming to the requisite anti-cartoon "rage," broadcasting
not only al-Qaradawi's sermon, but also kindred statements by other
Muslim notables. The Qatari university lecturer Ali Muhi Al-Din
Al-Qardaghi described the cartoons as part of a "Crusader Zionist
campaign" launched by "a Jew in Denmark."[3] In a sermon delivered at
a Damascus mosque before a crowd chanting "Death to Israel! Death
to America!", Hamas leader Khaled Mash'al urged European countries
to "hurry up and apologize." Noting that the Muslim *ummah* would
soon "sit on the throne of the world," he warned, "Apologize today,
before remorse will do you no good."[4]

Spurred on by al-Qaradawi and Al Jazeera, Muslim protests
against the cartoons were raging around the world by the time of
Calderoli's fateful television appearance on February 15. Danish dip-

2.   MEMRI (Middle East Media Research Institute), Special Dispatch no. 1089,
February 9, 2006. See too Jytte Klausen, "Muslims Representing Muslims in Europe,"
in Abdulkader H. Sinno, *Muslims in Western Politics* (Bloomington: Indiana University
Press, 2009), p. 105.

3.   See "Qatari University Lecturer Ali Muhi Al-Din Al-Qardaghi: Muhammad
Cartoon Is a Jewish Attempt to Divert European Hatred from Jews to Muslims," MEMRI
TV, clip #1030.

4.   See "Hamas Leader Khaled Mash'al at a Damascus Mosque: The Nation of
Islam Will Sit at the Throne of the World and the West Will Be Full of Remorse When
It Is Too Late," MEMRI TV, clip #1024.

lomatic representations had been set on fire in Beirut, Damascus and Tehran. "When they recognize our rights," Calderoli said, alluding to the protestors, "I'll take off the shirt." His act of defiance was widely reported in the Arab media, including on Al Jazeera.[5]

*Roberto Calderoli wearing a t-shirt with a cartoon
of Mohammed printed on it, February 15, 2006.*

But it appears to have been a more traditional means of communication in the Arab world that brought Benghazi's faithful out onto the street two days later: Friday prayers at the local mosques. February 17, 2006 was a Friday. According to an eyewitness account, in the late afternoon thousands of young men descended upon the Italian consulate from the mosques.[6]

---

5. In addition to citing Al-Jazeera, the Italian daily *Corriere della Sera* cites a figure of over 200 Arabic-language newspapers that carried the story. *Corriere della Sera*, February 17, 2006.

6. *Corriere della Sera*, February 18, 2006.

After attempting to break down the front door, rioters set fire to the building. One of the persons trapped inside was the wife of Italian consul general Giovanni Pirrello. "We feared for our lives," she would recall.[7] In an amateur video of the assault, rioters can be heard yelling "*Allahu Akbar!*" as the building burns.[8] One rioter menacingly waves a machete.

The Italian consulate in Benghazi on fire, February 17, 2006.

A further attempt to break into the building occurred on Friday night, after the fire had subsided or was put out. While speaking by phone with an Italian journalist, a consulate employee still trapped inside related what was happening. "Do you hear those pounding

---

7.   *Corriere della Sera*, February 18, 2006.
8.   The video can be viewed at http://www.youtube.com/watch?v=rIMBR17KV0U.

noises?" he said, "They are trying to break down the door."[9] Another amateur video, this one filmed at night, appears to document the second attempt. Cries of "*Allahu Akbar!*" ring out as a group of young men pound against the door with a battering ram.[10]

Sometime in between the first and the second attempt, Libyan police evacuated Pirrello, his wife, and the bulk of the remaining consulate personnel. It was perhaps at this time that police opened fire on the rioters, killing a reported eleven people and wounding many others. According to the Italian consul general, the police had first attempted to disperse the rioters using tear gas, but had been overwhelmed by their sheer numbers.[11]

Rioting would continue in Benghazi through the weekend and into the following Monday, when the rioters would turn their attention to symbols of Christianity, laying waste the city's only church. "No one could stop [them] . . .," a witness to the attack on the church observed, "They want to teach the crusaders a lesson."[12] A report from Vatican Radio spoke of two priests managing "to hide and miraculously to escape from the enraged mob."[13] Both the church and a Franciscan convent attached to it would be set ablaze.[14]

On Wednesday, February 23, a triumphant video clip celebrating "Italy's defeat" appeared on an al-Qaeda-linked Internet forum. The video documented the damage inflicted on the Italian consulate in Benghazi. According to reports in the Italian press, it began with a written exhortation to "Kill the infidels." A comment in the forum celebrated Benghazi as "one of the Libyan cities most famous for jihad." The remark suggests that the author already knew what

---

9. *L'Unità*, February 18, 2006.
10. The video can be viewed at http://www.youtube.com/watch?v=9Q-wbcT9wcg.
11. *L'Unità*, February 18, 2006.
12. *Corriere della Sera*, February 21, 2006.
13. Radio Vaticana, February 22, 2006.
14. See, for instance, "Incendiati una chiesa e un convento di francescani in Libia", *Zenit* (Catholic news agency), February 26, 2006. From the reports in the Italian press, it would appear that the church and the convent were the targets of repeated attacks—so too was the Italian consulate, even after its abandonment by the consulate personnel.

American counterterrorism analysts would only discover a year-and-a-half later, when captured al-Qaeda personnel records revealed a heavy flow of jihadists from Benghazi to Iraq to join the late Abu Musab al-Zarqawi's Iraqi al-Qaeda affiliate. The soundtrack to the Benghazi video is reported to have used some of the same religious chants used in the propaganda videos of the al-Zarqawi group.[15]

As indicated by the date chosen for the 2011 protests, the deaths of the rioters at the Italian consulate five years earlier represented one of the major simmering grievances driving the eastern Libyan opposition to Qaddafi. In an interview that he gave to the French weekly *Le Journal du Dimanche* in March 2011, Qaddafi would recognize the fault of the police and regret that they had not used rubber bullets or water cannons to disperse the rioters.[16]

Italians would not soon forget the trauma of the 2006 Benghazi riots. This helps to explain the Italian government's initial refusal to support a military intervention in Libya and its reluctance to recognize the Benghazi-based National Transitional Council. Alluding to the creation of an "Islamic Emirate" in eastern Libya in the earliest days of the rebellion, then Italian foreign minister Franco Frattini warned, "We don't know more [about it]. But we know that they are dangerous. There are elements of al-Qaeda there."[17]

It is one of the many ironies of the Libya War that Italy would eventually be pressured into joining its NATO partners in providing air support to a rebellion that was largely sparked by measures taken by the Libyan government to protect Italian citizens from a lynch mob. It is a measure of how thoroughly misinformed the American public

---

15. From the Italian reports, it appears that the exhortation to "kill the infidels" was written in a sort of pidgin English mixed with Arabic. The Turin-based *La Stampa* rendered it, for instance, as "Kill the Kafron for muslem " (*La Stampa*, February 24, 2006). "Kafron" is presumably an attempted anglicization of the the Arabic word *Kuffar*, meaning "infidels" or "non-believers." See too *La Repubblica* (online), February 23, 2006 and *Il Giornale*, February 24, 2006.

16. *Le Journal du Dimanche*, March 5, 2011.

17. Interview with Franco Frattini, *Corriere della Sera*, February 23, 2011.

was about the Libya crisis that shortly after the start of the NATO bombing campaign, Secretary of State Hillary Clinton could with a straight face include Italy in a list of NATO countries that had allegedly pushed for military intervention, because it was "in their vital national interest."[18] Never mind that Italy had concluded a "friendship agreement" with Libya only three years earlier and received nearly 40% of its oil imports from Libya.

But undoubtedly the greatest irony of the Libya War is that the NATO bombing campaign was led by none other than Anders Fogh Rasmussen: the same Anders Fogh Rasmussen who in his capacity as then Danish prime minister had drawn the ire of Yusuf al-Qaradawi and other Muslim activists by defending the right of *Jyllands-Posten* to publish the "Mohammed cartoons."

On October 12, 2005, less than two weeks after the original publication of the cartoons, eleven ambassadors and representatives from Muslim countries and the Palestinian territories addressed a letter to Prime Minister Rasmussen, urging him to call *Jyllands-Posten* to order and requesting an "urgent meeting." In his written response, Rasmussen underlined that "freedom of expression is the very foundation of the Danish democracy."[19] Not only did he decline to intervene in the matter. He refused even to meet with the signatories of the appeal.

"This is a matter of principle," Rasmussen explained at the time, "I will not meet with them because it is so crystal clear what principles Danish democracy is built upon that there is no reason to do so." "As prime minister, I have no power whatsoever to limit the press," he added, "nor do I want such power."[20]

Barely six years later, on October 30, 2011, Rasmussen, at this point serving as secretary general of NATO, declared the NATO operation in Libya to be one of "the most successful" in the history

18. *Meet the Press*, NBC, March 27, 2011.
19. Anders Fogh Rasmussen, letter to eleven ambassadors and representatives, October 21, 2005.
20. *The Copenhagen Post*, October 25, 2005.

of the alliance. He did not mention that this "success" facilitated the victory of the very forces that in 2006 had made "crystal clear" that they do not share his principles.

Ten days earlier, on October 20, rebel forces shot and killed a captive Muammar al-Qaddafi. Before doing so, they subjected him to a savage beating, much of it documented on video. The capture of Qaddafi had been made possible by a massive NATO aerial attack on his convoy, as it attempted to flee the besieged city of Sirte. The fact that the convoy was leaving the city in broad daylight lends plausibility to rumors that a deal had been struck to offer Qaddafi and his remaining forces safe-passage in exchange for the surrender of the city.

As the secretary general of NATO would know, the killing of Qaddafi in captivity was a war crime per Western conceptions of the laws and customs of war. But the rebels who first tormented and then murdered Qaddafi would undoubtedly have been less interested in the niceties of the Geneva Conventions than in the rulings on Islamic jurisprudence of Sharia scholars like Yusuf al-Qaradawi—Rasmussen's old nemesis from the days of the "cartoon jihad." Per Qaradawi, the summary execution of Qaddafi was not only *halal*—permitted—it was obligatory. In a *fatwa* issued on Al-Jazeera on February 21, shortly after the outbreak of the unrest in Libya, he called on "whoever can fire a bullet" to kill the Libyan leader.[21] It was, in effect, the fulfillment of al-Qaradawi's *fatwa* that brought to a close Rasmussen's "most successful" operation in NATO's history.

---

21. "Leading Sunni Scholar Sheik Yousuf Al-Qaradhawi Issues Fatwa to Army to Kill Libyan Leader Mu'ammar Al-Qadhafi," MEMRI TV, clip #2819.

CHAPTER 3

Black Flags in Benghazi— and Beyond

On October 23, 2011, three days after the fall of Sirte and the murder of Muammar al-Qaddafi, National Transitional Council chair Mustafa Abdul Jalil officially declared the "liberation" of Libya at a ceremony in Benghazi. Within days of Jalil's declaration, the black flag of al-Qaeda was spotted flying atop the Benghazi courthouse: the symbolic cradle of the anti-Qaddafi rebellion. British Prime Minister David Cameron and then French President Nicolas Sarkozy had feted the Libyan rebellion from the steps of the courthouse barely five weeks earlier. The appearance of the flag provoked surprise and consternation among American commentators. But, as will be seen further on, it should not have come as any surprise.

Defenders of the rebellion attempted to minimize the significance of the flag sighting, insisting that the hoisting of the flag had been an isolated incident or even suggesting that pictures of it had been photo-shopped. But the flag atop the courthouse was not the only al-Qaeda flag to be seen in Benghazi in the week after Libya's "liberation." As demonstrated by photographic and video evidence posted on Arabic-language Internet forums and YouTube pages, the Benghazi waterfront had in fact been awash with al-Qaeda flags in those days.

Astonishingly, some of the photos even made their way into the American press—apparently without, however, the responsible editors realizing what the photos show. Thus one such photo appeared in the *New York Times* accompanied merely by the following—relatively innocuous—caption: "Benghazi on Friday, several hundred men rallied to demand the application of Islamic law, or Shariah, in Libya. That could clear the way for polygamy."[1] No mention was made—much less explanation given—for the al-Qaeda flags that can clearly be seen fluttering over the demonstrators' heads.

October 2011: Demonstrators with al-Qaeda flags on the Benghazi waterfront.
(© REUTERS/Esam Al-Fetori)

Video of the same demonstration uploaded by local users onto Arabic language YouTube pages shows at least hundreds, if not indeed thousands, of men gathered on the Benghazi waterfront with al-Qaeda

---

1. *New York Times*, October 29, 2011.

flags spread densely throughout the crowd. The videos were posted by Tawasul and Tadhamun [Solidarity]: two online media that sprung up in Benghazi in the wake of the rebellion.[2] The demonstration took place on October 28th: five days after the proclaimed "liberation" of Libya.

The flag flown by the demonstrators on the Benghazi waterfront is, more precisely, the flag made famous by the late Abu Musab al-Zarqawi's al-Qaeda in Iraq, which was originally known as *Jama'at al-Tawhid wal-Jihad*: the "Monotheism and Jihad Group." Al-Zarqawi pledged fealty to Osama bin Laden and officially declared his group an al-Qaeda affiliate in October 2004. Following al-Zarqawi's death in June 2006, the group merged into the so-called Islamic State of Iraq, which continues to use the flag to this day.

The flag that flew over the Benghazi courthouse is an early version of the Zarqawi group's flag. The black flag carried by the Benghazi demonstrators is the standard version that became al-Qaeda in Iraq's trademark via numerous videos immortalizing the group's grisly exploits. These "exploits" included beheadings of Americans and other foreigners in Iraq and summary executions of Iraqi security personnel. The flag features the *shahada* or Islamic declaration of faith—"There is no god but God [Allah], Mohammed is his messenger"—and a white circle in the middle said to represent Mohammed's "seal." In the standard version of the flag, the words "Mohammed is his messenger" appear in black at the interior of the seal. The same flag is used in the banner artwork of several well-known al-Qaeda-linked jihadist Internet forums.[3]

The demonstrators on the Benghazi waterfront also flew an "inverted" white version of the flag with a black circle in the middle.

---

2.   The Tawasul footage is available at http://www.youtube.com/watch?v=U9-tv4BNTgw. Higher quality Tadhamun footage is available at http://www.youtube.com/watch?v=Gjax1Qx6OQU and http://www.youtube.com/watch?v=qF3snH8n9j0.
3.   For examples, see "Top Arabic Jihadi forums," Internet Haganah, June 5, 2011.

The use of the black and white versions of the al-Qaeda flag mirrors the symbolism of the so-called caliphate flag, which likewise exists in black and white versions. The black version of the caliphate flag—a solid black flag with the *shahada* in white—was the first flag to serve as al-Qaeda's banner, prior to the Zarqawi group's innovation. As opposed to the black flag of jihad, the white caliphate flag represents Islamic rule. It was, for instance, used by the Taliban's "Islamic Emirate of Afghanistan."

2007: Execution of Iraqi security personnel in front of al-Qaeda Flag.

But it was not only demonstrators who raised the al-Qaeda flag after the "liberation" of Libya. Some of the very troops with whom NATO allied in order to secure that "liberation" did so as well.

Indeed, already during the siege of Sirte, a correspondent for the Algerian newspaper *Echorouk* reported seeing rebel troops flying "the black banners and flags of 'There is no God but Allah and Mohammed is his messenger.'" A photo accompanying the report showed what appeared to be a rebel pick-up truck with a heavy machine gun mounted on the back. A black caliphate flag flutters over the vehicle. By its own count, NATO conducted hundreds of airstrikes on Sirte prior to its fall. Rebel artillery, like the weapon seen in the *Echorouk* photo, pounded the city from its outskirts. The spotting of the caliphate flags was not, incidentally, the only notable sighting that the *Echorouk* correspondent made: According to his report, two British soldiers were present on the ground, helping the rebel gunners to hit their marks.[4]

In March 2012, five months after the fall of Sirte, a video providing graphic corroboration of the *Echorouk* report emerged on an Arabic-language YouTube page. The title of the clip is "Al-Qaeda *takfiris* and their black flag in the streets of Sirte 03-23-2012"[5] *Takfir* is the act of declaring a fellow Muslim to be an apostate. *Takfiris* are those who issue such denunciations. The practice is central to al-Qaeda ideology, which claims to defend the "purity" of original Islam against a wide variety of subsequent heresies and perversions. The denunciation of an individual or sect by *takfiris* is tantamount to an incitement to violence against them. As will be seen in a later chapter, one notable target of *takfir* on the part of al-Qaeda and like-minded extremist groups was none other than Muammar al-Qaddafi.

The March 2012 video shows a column of over two dozen trucks, many of them with heavy machine guns mounted on the back. The big guns are manned by masked gunners. Armed occupants of the

---

4.   The sightings by the *Echorouk* correspondent were first reported in English by the now regrettably dormant *Roads to Iraq* blog. See "British forces and Al-Qaeda fighters side-by-side in Libya," Roads to Iraq, October 22, 2011. An English-language Al-Jazeera report, which, in effect, celebrates the fall of Sirte, likewise clearly shows a jeep full of triumphant rebel fighters flying a black caliphate flag. See Al Jazeera English, "Al Jazeera's Tony Birtley reports from Sirte on Gaddafi's capture," October 20, 2011 (consultable at http://www.youtube.com/watch?v=ujP5wzMV4Nw).

5.   Available at http://www.youtube.com/watch?v=ifQr62smdTI. The procession documented in the clip appears to have taken place on the same day as the original posting: March 23, 2012.

vehicles shout *"Allahu Akbar!"* as they roll past the vantage point of the camera. Almost all the trucks are flying the black flag of al-Qaeda. Some of them even sport decals of a black map of Libya inscribed with the *shahada* and a white "seal of Mohammed" in the middle. The symbolic claiming of Libya for al-Qaeda and its ideology could hardly be more obvious. Even some of the fire trucks bringing up the rear of the procession sport decals of the al-Qaeda flag.

Al-Qaeda flag and rebel gunner in Sirte, March 2012
(Note the map of Libya in the colors of the al-Qaeda flag on the windshield)

The word "Sirte" in large red Arabic script is clearly visible on a decal on the doors of two of the vehicles. (Smaller script is illegible. It perhaps refers to a local brigade or to a local public utility from which the vehicles were seized.) The identical decal is also visible on the door of the vehicle in the *Echorouk* photo.

The original poster of the video identifies the leader of the unit as Wisam Hamid from the city of Derna. The poster is, incidentally, clearly a fan neither of al-Qaeda nor of the February 17 revolution. Concerning Wisam Hamid, the description specifies further: "This base individual, son of a whore, is 35 years old and very large units belong to him in the East, as far as Kufra in the South, and West as far as Sirte . . . ."

Contemporary reports in Arabic media, including the local Benghazi-based pro-rebellion media, identified Wisam bin Hamid as the commander of the rebel forces that laid siege to Sirte.[6] This means that whether directly or indirectly, it was with bin Hamid that NATO command was coordinating its aerial operations. It also means that it was bin Hamid's men who seized and slaughtered Muammar al-Qaddafi following the NATO bombardment on the morning of October 20, 2011.

Many months later, in June and July of 2012, bin Hamid turned up in Western news reports at the head of a so-called Libya Shield Brigade, which had been dispatched by Libya's interim government from Benghazi to remote Kufra, deep in the Sahara nearly 600 miles to the South. The ostensible purpose of the deployment was to quell unrest that had broken out between a local Arab tribe, the Zuwayya, and a black African tribe, the Toubou. In a June 30 French-language AFP report, Hamid's brigade was even described as a "peace-keeping force."[7]

But Wisam bin Hamid is an odd sort of "peacekeeper." Only weeks earlier, the very same AFP reported that his forces were pounding Toubou neighborhoods of the city with heavy artillery.[8] Tribal chief Issa Abdelmajid accused the brigade of trying to "exterminate" the Toubou. The hostility of the Libya Shield forces to the Toubou might have its roots in *Takfiri* ideology. Although the Toubou have been Islamized in recent times, they reportedly continue to mix their

---

6. *Ash-Sharq al-Awsat*, October 16, 2011; Tadhamun [Solidarity], "Interview with Wisam bin Hamid," October 12, 2011, available at http://www.youtube.com/watch?v=oCcz6wrZP-g.
7. "Libye: 47 morts en 3 jours dans des affrontements à Koufra, dans le Sud-Est," AFP, June 30, 2012.
8. "23 killed in two days of south Libya clashes", AFP, June 10, 2012.

version of Islam with many pre-Islamic animist beliefs and practices.[9] Indeed, according to one theory, the very name *Kufra* represents a disparaging allusion to the Toubou and their traditionally non-Islamic ways. It appears to be derived from the Arabic word *Kuffar:* meaning "unbelievers" or "infidels."

A report from a Norwegian NGO notes that even after a ceasefire had been negotiated in Kufra, "Libyan Shield militiamen drove around town flying the Prophet Mohammed's black flag of jihad from their vehicles' aerials."[10] The allusion to "the Prophet Mohammed's black flag of jihad" is a euphemism. Mohammed's flag appears to have been a solid black flag without any inscription on it. Libya Shield forces fly the modern flags of jihad.

Brigade units were reportedly first deployed to Kufra in February 2012—perhaps not coincidentally at a time when there was chatter on pro-Qaddafi websites about "green resistance" forces, i.e. Qaddafi loyalists, moving back into the town.[11] Extensive footage from mid-March shows Libya Shield vehicles in the region of Kufra flying both the new red-black-and-green Libyan national flag and crude black "caliphate" flags, like those flown by Wisam bin Hamid's forces at the siege of Sirte.[12]

Decals on the vehicles feature the red-and-gold Libya Shield logo. Underscoring the official sponsorship of the brigade by the Libyan government, Arabic writing on the logo reads "Ministry of Defense—Libya Shield Forces." Some of the vehicles also bear decals reading "The Martyrs of Free Libya Brigade." As references in local

---

9. See, for instance, Andrew B. Smith, *African Herders* (Walnut Creek, CA: Altamira Press, 2005), pp. 133 ff.

10. Nicolas Pelham, "Rivalries for Authority in Libya", NOREF: Norwegian Peacebuilding Resource Center, June 2012.

11. In an interview with the Associated Press, NTC chair Mustapha Abdul-Jalil tacitly acknowledged the accuracy of these reports, cryptically noting that Qaddafi loyalists were "spreading sedition" in Kufra. See "Libyan Leader Acknowledges Mistakes," Associated Press, February 22, 2012.

12. For examples of such video evidence, see http://www.youtube.com/watch?v=Yv4gGXKu-wY (starting at the 0:43 mark) and http://www.youtube.com/watch?v=xlsC3YDax4E (throughout). The videos were posted by pro-rebellion sources.

online media make clear, "The Martyrs of Free Libya Brigade" was the original brigade commanded by Wisam Bin Hamid during the anti-Qaddafi uprising and prior to the founding of Libya Shield.

Libya Shield forces flying black jihadist flag, near al-Kufra, March 2012

Libya Shield vehicle flying black jihadist flag, al-Kufra, March 2012

In a video posted online on April 13, 2012 by Free Kufra News, Libya Shield spokesman Hafez al-Aquri holds forth on the Kufra conflict. Free Kufra News is a Kufra-based counterpart to pro-rebellion

Benghazi-based online media like Tawasul and Tadhamun. According to the Arabic text accompanying the post, al-Aquri is not only the spokesman of Libya Shield, but also himself one of the "senior commanders" of the brigade. In the clip, he is seated at a desk and swivels back and forth in his chair as he speaks. Behind him, hanging from a bookcase, there is a large gold-fringed al-Qaeda flag.[13]

Libya Shield Brigade spokesman Hafez al-Aquri
in front of al-Qaeda flag, April 2012

On June 7, 2012—around the time that Wisam bin Hamid's forces were shelling Toubou neighborhoods in Kufra—civilian demonstrators and *mujahideen* forces came together in Benghazi for a large "rally in support of Islamic *sharia*." The proceedings included a motorized military parade. Nearly thirty minutes of footage posted online by Tawasul shows truckloads of *mujahideen* rolling down the Benghazi waterfront, guns and RPGs in hand.[14] Many of the trucks have big

---

13. Video available at http://www.youtube.com/watch?v=qrcFCZ-mYd4.
14. Two Tawasul videos documenting the proceedings are available at http://www.youtube.com/watch?v=wRmdtRQf4b8 and http://www.youtube.com/watch?v=hLM5O5LFvP8. The procession was obviously a very major event in Benghazi and could hardly have been missed by anyone present in downtown. But the only English-

guns—machine guns, anti-aircraft weapons, and rocket-launchers—mounted on the back. The red-and-gold Libya Shield logo is clearly visible on some of the vehicles.

Al-Qaeda flags and caliphate flags are everywhere. A small group of *mujahideen* rhythmically chants *"Allahu Akbar."* One fighter wears a black al-Qaeda headband with a white "seal of Mohammed" in the middle. A civilian (as far as one can tell) runs amidst the vehicles carrying an al-Qaeda flag in his outstretched hand. Even children get in on the act. Two little boys, the smaller one not older than four, lean out the window of a pick-up truck. The toddler wears a black headband with the *shahada* written on it in white. The older boy, perhaps his big brother, wears an al-Qaeda headband and waves a caliphate flag. A gunner mans a heavy machine gun mounted on the back of the truck. A little girl in another vehicle shouts *"Allahu Akbar"* out the window.

On the windshields of several of the trucks, the same decal is visible as was visible on some of the trucks that rolled through Sirte two months earlier: a black map of Libya with a white "seal of Mohammed" in the middle—Libya in the form of an al-Qaeda flag.

Military parade with al-Qaeda flags and decals, Benghazi, June 2012

---

language news service to have covered it appears to have been the Iranian international broadcaster Press TV.

CHAPTER 4

Libya's Al-Qaeda: The Libyan Islamic Fighting Group

The appearance of al-Qaeda flags in Benghazi after Libya's "liberation" should not have come as any surprise, because from the very start of the Libyan rebellion, it was well-known in counter-terrorism circles that the eastern Libyan heartland of the rebellion was a hotbed of support for al-Qaeda. It was not only Italian foreign minister Franco Frattini who knew that "there are elements of al-Qaeda there." American officials knew it too.

More precisely, they knew that Libya's eastern Cyrenaica region—and, in particular, the northeastern seaboard—had been a hotbed of support for the Iraqi branch of al-Qaeda and its jihad against American forces and their Iraqi government allies. The coastal city of Benghazi is the capital of Cyrenaica.

In October 2007, coalition forces in Iraq captured a stash of al-Qaeda personnel records during a raid near the town of Sinjar not far from the Syrian border. The "Sinjar Records" document the origins of the foreign recruits that joined Al-Qaeda in Iraq between August 2006 and August 2007. An analysis of the records by the Combating Terrorism Center at West Point came to a hitherto unexpected conclusion. Unsurprisingly, the largest contingent of recruits came from Saudi Arabia. In per capita terms, however, the most important supplier of al-Qaeda recruits turned out to be none other than Libya.[1] The "vast majority" of the Libyan al-Qaeda recruits, moreover, came precisely from Libya's fractious northeast, long known to harbor the most militant domestic opposition to Qaddafi.

Two eastern Libyan cities in particular stood out in the statistics: Benghazi and Derna. Both cities would figure among the first to rise up against Qaddafi in February 2011, and both would remain strongholds of the rebellion, with Derna taking on an importance disproportionate to its small size. If Benghazi was the political capital of the rebellion, Derna appears in many ways to have served as its military nerve center. In light of the data compiled from the Sinjar Records, it is not difficult to understand why.

Among all the cities and towns to provide recruits to al-Qaeda in Iraq during the year covered by the records, Derna topped the table with 53 al-Qaeda volunteers: two more than the second place finisher, the Saudi capital Riyadh. To put in perspective the degree of fanaticism that this implies, consider that with merely 80,000 inhabitants Derna's population is just 1/50th that of Riyadh. As the West Point analysts noted, in per capita terms, Derna thus contributed "far and away" the greatest number of fighters to al-Qaeda's Iraqi jihad. Small wonder, then, that the city's residents would go on to distinguish themselves just a few years later in the jihad against Qaddafi.

The Libyan al-Qaeda recruits appear to have taken particular pride in volunteering for "martyrdom" assignments, i.e. suicide missions. Of the 61 Libyans who listed their "work" on the personnel sheets, fully 85%, perhaps as testimony to their faith, volunteered to die.

---

1. See *Al-Qa'ida's Foreign Fighters in Iraq: A First Look at the Sinjar Records* (Combating Terrorism Center at West Point: December 2007).

But Libya did not only serve as an important source of manpower for al-Qaeda in Iraq. Libya also had its own al-Qaeda affiliate: the Libyan Islamic Fighting Group (LIFG). The LIFG had long aimed to topple the rule of the "apostate" Qaddafi. The group had indeed attempted to assassinate the Libyan leader on several occasions in the 1990s. One such attempt is reported to have taken place in Derna in 1994. The assassination plot is said to have been led by a certain Abu-Abdallah al-Sadiq, a Tripoli native who took refuge in eastern Libya after fighting in the anti-Soviet jihad in Afghanistan in the late 1980s. When the LIFG abandoned its hitherto strictly clandestine existence and published its first communiqué in 1995, al-Sadiq emerged as the head of the organization.[2]

Derna and the surrounding region clearly served as the group's base of operations and would consequently be the target of Libyan military campaigns aimed at wiping out the group. According to the account given on the LIFG's own, now defunct, website almuqatila. com, some 30,000 Libyan troops besieged the city in 1997.[3]

In November 2007, al-Qaeda chief ideologue and current leader, Ayman al-Zawahiri, announced the official incorporation of the LIFG into the al-Qaeda network. But, according to numerous concordant sources, the two groups already had a longstanding relationship forged through more than a decade of close cooperation in jihadist sanctuaries in Sudan and Afghanistan.[4]

Osama bin Laden had moved his operations from Afghanistan to Sudan after the close of the anti-Soviet jihad. When, under US pressure, Sudanese authorities expelled bin Laden and his followers

---

2. That al-Sadiq personally led the 1994 assassination plot is claimed by several sources. It appears to have first been noted by Moshe Terdman in "The Libyan Islamic Fighting Group," GLORIA Center, PRISM Occasional Papers, Volume 3, no. 2 (June 2005). Terdman cites in turn the LIFG website almuqatila.com.

3. Cited in Evan Kohlmann, "Dossier: Libyan Islamic Fighting Group (LIFG)," (NEFA Foundation: October 2007), p. 10.

4. For an extensive collection of evidence, see Kohlmann, "Dossier: Libyan Islamic Fighting Group (LIFG)."

in 1996, the Taliban welcomed them back to Afghanistan. The LIFG followed virtually the same itinerary—except that, as a consequence of protestations by Qaddafi, the LIFG contingent was thrown out of Sudan one year earlier. Wherever al-Qaeda set up shop so too did the LIFG.

Having been damaged by Libyan military operations and despairing of popular support, by the late 1990s the LIFG was essentially an exile organization devoted to global jihad operating under the al-Qaeda umbrella.[5] In Afghanistan, it both ran its own jihadist training facilities and shared facilities with al-Qaeda. The two organizations did not only cooperate: they were, in effect, intertwined.

The LIFG was thus one of the select few Islamic extremist organizations to be designated as an al-Qaeda affiliate by the U.N. Security Council already in October 2001, in the immediate aftermath of the 9/11 attacks. The U.N. listing notes that the LIFG earned this distinction by virtue of "participating in the financing, planning, facilitating, preparing or perpetrating of acts or activities by, in conjunction with, under the name of, on behalf or in support of . . . Al-Qaida, Usama bin Laden and the Taliban."[6]

In his recorded November 2007 statement announcing the LIFG's even closer union with al-Qaeda, al-Zawahiri addressed his glad tidings to the LIFG's leader, "the emir of the *mujahideen*, the patient and steadfast Abu-Abdallah al-Sadiq," as well as to the organization's chief ideologue and religious authority, "his eminence, the mujahid scholar Abu al-Munthir al-Saadi." Al-Zawahiri will undoubtedly have known both men well from the two group's fertile period of collaboration in Afghanistan under Taliban rule. Al-Munthir had been so highly

---

5.   On the LIFG's lack of popular support, see the admission by LIFG spokesman Omer Rashid: "We cannot say that the Libyan people in general have passed beyond the stage of sentiments to the stage of action . . . we are witnessing the absence of the role of the people from confronting Qaddhafi and his regime . . . .' Cited in Kohlmann, "Dossier: Libyan Islamic Fighting Group (LIFG)," p. 10.

6.   UN Security Council 1267 Committee, Narrative Summary of Reasons for Listing: Libyan Islamic Fighting Group.

esteemed by his hosts that Taliban leader Mullah Omar is reported to have named him "The Sheikh of the Arabs in Afghanistan."[7]

At the time of al-Zawahiri's announcement, both al-Sadiq and al-Munthir were being held prisoner in Libya—thanks, namely, to American counter-terrorism operations and, in particular, the controversial program of "extraordinary rendition." Extraordinary rendition involved the capturing of terror suspects and their transfer for interrogation and "safe-keeping" to countries that were cooperating with US authorities in the "war on terror."

Little known to most Americans, by the middle of the last decade, the Libya of America's erstwhile *bête noire*, Muammar al-Qaddafi, had become an American ally. As late as August 2009, a since-leaked American State Department cable was describing Libya as indeed "a critical ally in US counterterrorism efforts" and "one of our primary partners in combating the flow of foreign fighters" (i.e. into Iraq).[8] The detention of al-Sadiq and al-Munthir was a product of this cooperation.

The 2001 American invasion of Afghanistan had smashed the country's network of jihadist training facilities and sent their occupants scattering. The massive American aerial assault on bin Laden's mountain complex at Tora Bora in mid-December was the decisive battle in this regard. Those of the "Afghan Arabs" who managed to survive fled to the Pakistani border. Many were picked up by Pakistani security forces and turned over to American authorities. Some of them ended up at Guantánamo Bay.

Others, who managed to evade capture, like Abu-Abdallah al-Sadiq, stayed on the run, spreading out to still more far-flung venues to avoid detection. It is not known when exactly al-Munthir left Afghanistan. But not long after the Battle of Tora Bora, he too was on the run.

---

7. Kohlmann, "Dossier: Libyan Islamic Fighting Group (LIFG),"citing the London-based Arabic daily *Al Hayat*.

8. "Scenesetter for Codel McCain's Trip To Libya," August 10, 2009.

American intelligence caught up with the two men in Southeast Asia in early 2004. Al-Sadiq and al-Munthir were detained in March 2004 in separate actions in Bangkok and Hong Kong respectively. They had previously been living in China: al-Sadiq in Beijing and al-Munthir in Guangzhou. But fearing that they were under surveillance, both were on the move yet again when they were detained. They would subsequently be transferred to Libyan custody.[9]

It is clear that American counter-terrorism investigators were able either to interrogate al-Sadiq and al-Munthir directly or to pass questions for them to their Libyan counterparts. It is equally clear that both men talked. Several leaked Defense Department "detainee assessments" regarding detainees held at Guantánamo Bay make explicit reference to information provided by al-Sadiq or al-Munthir or both.[10] In March 2010, six years after their transfer to Libyan custody, the two men were released as part of an amnesty agreement with the Libyan government.

Nowadays, al-Sadiq goes by the name Abdul-Hakim Belhadj. In August 2011, following the fall of Tripoli, he would emerge as the commander of the rebel forces that had taken control of the Libyan capital and the city's new military governor.

Al-Munthir is nowadays known as Sami al-Saadi. As befitting a spiritual authority and "scholar," as Ayman al-Zawahiri described him, al-Munthir appears not to have participated directly in combat. Indeed, Libyan authorities appear to have made sure of this by incarcerating

---

9. The above is based on the two men's own representations in lawsuits filed against the governments of Great Britain and Hong Kong. See Leigh Day & Co Solicitors, "Letter of Claim Re: Mr Abdel Hakim Belhadj and Ms Fatima Bouchar, Detention in Bangkok and Rendition to Libya in March 2004", November 7, 2011; and Ho, Tse Wai & Partners, "Claim on behalf of Mr Sami Al-Saadi against HKSARG" (letter to Hong Kong Department of Justice), June 12, 2012.

10. See, for instance, JTF-GTMO Detainee Assessment: Ismael Ali Bakush, January 22, 2008: "Senior LIFG members al-Sadiq and al-Sadi [i.e. al-Munthir] identified detainee as an explosives trainer for the LIFG."

him again shortly after the outbreak of the rebellion.[11] But, as will be seen below in chapter 9, he was as much as anyone the father of the Libyan rebellion.

The Libyan jihadist "insider" Noman Benotman has placed al-Sadiq/Belhadj at Tora Bora with Osama bin Laden in late 2001, as American and allied special forces closed in. On Benotman's account, in light of the militarily hopeless situation, the LIFG commander withdrew with his troops to Pakistan at this time.[12]

After the fall of Tripoli, the Spanish daily *ABC* contacted five longtime LIFG members and close associates of Belhadj. The Libyan jihadist veterans told *ABC* that Belhadj personally ran an LIFG "guesthouse" in Afghanistan. "We were around two hundred [men] and we all received military training before going to the front," one Mohammed Kreir recalled. "We are educated people and well-prepared—that's why we've played an important role in this revolution," Kreir added, alluding to the rebellion against Qaddafi.[13]

One Tareq Muftah Durman noted that Belhadj had had "a direct line to Osama bin Laden." Durman insisted, however, that the Libyan jihadists "never shared Osama's strategy."

11. Al-Saadi himself claims that he spent the bulk of the rebellion in prison in Tripoli. See Ho, Tse Wai & Partners, "Claim on behalf of Mr Sami Al-Saadi against HKSARG," June 12, 2012.

12. See Camille Tawil, *The Other Face of Al-Qaeda* (Quilliam Foundation, 2010), p. 23.

13. *ABC*, September 9, 2011.

CHAPTER 5

The LIFG and the Madrid Train Bombings

If the LIFG's long history of collaboration with al-Qaeda in Sudan and Afghanistan was not already enough, Spanish police investigations into the 2004 Madrid train bombings provide still more reason to doubt that the Libyan jihadists "never shared Osama's strategy." Telephone records obtained by Spanish investigators indicate that in early January 2004, fugitive LIFG chief Abdul-Hakim Belhadj was in contact with a certain Serhane ben Abdelmajid Fakhet, aka "*El Tunecino*" or "The Tunisian." Fakhet was the leader of the terror cell that carried out the train bombings two months later.

The telephone records show that Fakhet placed calls to two Chinese telephone numbers belonging to Belhadj. They likewise show that shortly thereafter Belhadj in turn placed numerous calls to both a mobile phone and a landline belonging to Fakhet's Jordanian colleague Abdallah Mohd Othman. It is known, moreover, that Fakhet himself made use of Othman's phone.[1]

Contacted by the Spanish daily *ABC* in September 2011, Tripoli's new military governor admitted to his contacts with both Fakhet and Othman. He insisted, however, that the purpose of the calls was to discuss "professional matters that had nothing to do with the [Madrid train] attacks."[2] In an interview with Spanish counter-terrorism expert Fernando Reinares in March 2010, Belhadj had previously described his relations with Fakhet as merely "social." Reinares met Belhadj in Tripoli one day after Belhadj was released from prison by the then Libyan authorities. When Reinares attempted to pursue the subject of his contacts with Fakhet, Belhadj cut off the conversation and "excused himself."[3]

In January 2004, Fakhet and Othman appear indeed to have been busy with "professional" matters. They were supposedly in the process of launching a furniture business together—although investigators found no evidence of any such business ever existing. At the end of the month, 3-4 weeks after the documented contacts with Belhadj, Fakhet placed a call from Othman's phone to a certain Ziyad al-Hashim in London. The purpose of the call was likewise to discuss the "furniture business," it would seem. As chance would have it, however, Fakhet's interlocutor was yet again a leading member of the Libyan Islamic Fighting Group. Spanish investigators have identified al-Hashim—aka "Mullah Shakir al-Ghaznawi," aka "Imad al-Libi" (Imad the Libyan)—as a member of the LIFG's "media committee."

---

1. *ABC* (Spanish daily), August 1, 2005. The revelations in the *ABC* article are drawn from a report that was prepared by the Spanish foreign intelligence service, the UCIE, and submitted to investigative judge Juan del Olmo.

2. *ABC*, December 17, 2011. Somewhat in contradiction to his other statements, Belhadj also told *ABC* that he did not take Fakhet's phone calls, since "the number seemed strange to me." (*ABC*, September 10, 2011.) The claim can hardly serve as an alibi, however, since he has, in any case, admitted to knowing Fakhet and to being in touch with him at the time.

3. "Las amistades libias de El Tunecino," *El País*, April 29, 2010.

A British immigration court ruling describes al-Hashim as a LIFG "propagandist and communicator" and notes that a website prepared by him demonstrated "his support for suicide operations." The website included songs and texts glorifying jihad and martyrdom.[4]

One such song, for instance, celebrated the "martyrs" of Kandahar: the city in southern Afghanistan where Mullah Omar's forces made their last stand in late 2001. With the blessings of Omar and the Taliban, Osama bin Laden and al-Qaeda had established their base of operations in Kandahar on their return to Afghanistan in the mid-1990s. Al-Hashim's website, which appears to have been launched or at least completed in November 2003, also contained propaganda material related to two of the other most notable frontlines of jihad at the time: Iraq and Palestine.

Another audio file on al-Hashim's website was titled simply "I am a terrorist." As odd as it may seem to Western observers, some al-Qaeda operatives and/or sympathizers have defiantly embraced the "terrorist" label that was placed on them by the West. The file from al-Hashim's website is perhaps the file that is known to have been downloaded to a computer in Milan in March 2004 by a certain Rabei Osman El Sayed, aka "Mohammed the Egyptian." Osman is suspected of being the mastermind behind the Madrid train bombings. Indeed, not long after the attacks, he would tell his disciple Rajah Yahia that the bombings were "my project" and that the perpetrators were "my dearest friends."[5] In November 2006, he would be found guilty by an Italian court of being "one of the top leaders of an international terrorist organization," which was implicated in the Madrid train bombings, among several other terror attacks.[6]

---

4. Special Immigration Appeals Commission judgment of April 27, 2007, Appeal No: SC/42 and 50/2005.

5. *Corriere della Sera*, June 9, 2004.

6. *Corriere della Sera*, February 16, 2007. In 2007, some 29 alleged accomplices of Fakhet and the other train bombers were put on trial in Spain. In what is undoubtedly the most shocking outcome of the trial, Spanish judges in October 2007 found Osman not guilty—this despite his own highly self-incriminating remarks and corroborative

Both witness testimony and material evidence connect Osman to Fakhet and other members of the Madrid terror cell—as indeed do Osman's own pronouncements. Osman lived in Madrid from summer 2001 until at least February 2003, during which time he is believed to have contributed to the radicalization of Fakhet and the other cell members. Spanish investigators, moreover, have uncovered evidence that he returned to Spain in January 2004, when the Madrid train plot was entering its final stages. According to Spanish prosecutors, Osman held meetings with cell members in "the last days of January"[7]—i.e. at the very time when Fakhet and Othman were contacting the LIFG's al-Hashim in London.

Italian investigators were able to reconstruct Osman's Internet usage beginning from a few weeks prior to the bombings until his arrest in June 2004. The police transcripts describe Osman listening at 5:33 am on March 31: "to a verse that obsessively repeats 'I am a terrorist . . . ,' followed by the voice of a little girl who asks for a suicide vest."[8] From the sketchy details available in the British immigration court ruling, it is apparent, incidentally, that al-Hashim's website also made allusion to such "child jihadists." One text, for instance, asked for children who will "make jihad" for the sake of Allah. A photograph of Palestinian children bore the caption "Islamic cubs of steadfastness and resistance in the face of Jewish pigs."

The record of Osman's Internet usage for May 8 includes a song that elucidates the Quranic background to jihadists' embrace of the "terrorist" label. "We are terrorists," the lyrics proclaim,

---

evidence of their veracity uncovered by both Italian and Spanish investigators. The Spanish judges, nonetheless, took it as "proven beyond doubt" that Osman was a member of "terrorist cells of a jihadist nature" and, furthermore, conceded that the established facts demonstrated that he had advance knowledge of the Madrid attacks. See Audencia National, *Sentencia número 65/2007*, October 31, 2007, p. 635.

7   Prosecutor's Revised Statement of Facts ("*Calificación Definitiva*"), June 4, 2007, p. 62 and notes 100 and 101.

8.   Excerpts from the police transcripts were published by the Italian newspaper *Corriere della Sera*. See "L'Internet radicale del terrorista Mohammed," *Corriere della Sera* (online), March 11, 2005.

> We want to make it known to everyone, from East to West, that
> we are terrorists. Because terrorism, as a verse of the Quran says,
> is something approved by God, who has said in his book: for the
> enemies of God, ready all your power to terrorize them . . . .[9]

The UK's Special Immigration Appeals Commission concluded
that al-Hashim was "a global jihadist with links to the Taleban and
Al Qa'eda." The court noted, furthermore, that he had "close links
to a number of senior LIFG members," including both Belhadj and
LIFG chief ideologue al-Munthir.[10]

When contacted by Fakhet in London at the end of January, al-
Hashim had only just arrived in the United Kingdom—namely, from
China, where, Spanish investigators have determined, he was with
Belhadj at the time of the LIFG leader's earlier consultations about the
"furniture business" with Fakhet and Othman. According to British
court records, al-Hashim has admitted to knowing Belhadj and that
Belhadj not only arranged for his accommodations in China, but also
provided him the Spanish passport in the name of "Hossein Abselam"
on which he travelled to the United Kingdom. But in keeping with
Belhadj's account of his relationship with Fakhet, al-Hashim insists
that his relations with Belhadj were likewise essentially "social" and/
or a matter of "business."[11]

Al-Hashim has also admitted to phone contacts—*nota bene*: in the
plural—with Fakhet, but insisted that they were similarly innocuous.
Spanish investigators have highlighted the fact that Fakhet placed
several calls to London after al-Hashim's arrival.

---

9. *Corriere della Sera* (online), March 11, 2005. The reference is to the Quran,
Surah 8:60.

10. Special Immigration Appeals Commission judgment of April 27, 2007, Appeal
No: SC/42 and 50/2005. In the British ruling, al-Hashim is identified merely as "DD"
and Belhadj is identified by his *nom de guerre* "al-Sadeq."

11. Special Immigration Appeals Commission judgment of April 27, 2007, Appeal
No: SC/42 and 50/2005.

Fakhet appears to have first contacted al-Hashim in London on or shortly after January 27 (the date of al-Hashim's arrival). Approximately six weeks later, early in the morning of March 11, 2004, 10 bombs exploded in four packed commuter trains in Madrid, killing 191 persons and injuring nearly two thousand others. Three weeks after that, Spanish police had tracked down the suspected perpetrators of the attacks to an apartment in the Leganés suburb of Madrid. On the evening of April 3rd, with police surrounding their hideout, the aspiring "furniture dealer," Serhane ben Abdelmajid Fakhet, and six other members of his terror cell blew up the apartment with dynamite, killing themselves and a Spanish police officer in the process. Several other police officers were wounded in the blast.

In the hours preceding the explosion, the trapped occupants of the apartment are known to have made numerous telephone calls, contacting both family members and jihadist notables around the world. The purpose of the calls to their fellow jihadists appears to have been to discuss their plans to evade capture by blowing up the apartment and to determine whether this novel use of suicide bombing was consistent with jihadist doctrine.[12] Suicide as such is forbidden in Islam, though radical clerics have justified *mujahideen* killing themselves in operations that procure a strategic benefit. Cell members called their families in order to say good-bye.

According to Spanish counter-terrorism expert Fernando Reinares, only *minutes* before the explosives were detonated, Fakhet placed a call to *yet another* high-ranking member of the Libyan Islamic Fighting Group in London. Reinares makes clear that the recipient of the call was not al-Hashim, but he does not say who it was. As we shall see in chapter 9, by the middle of the last decade, the United Kingdom had become a safe haven for many LIFG members, including some of the organization's leaders.

---

12. *El Mundo*, May 11, 2004 (among others).

The Libyan jihadist "insider" Noman Benotman has told Reinares that he was with Fakhet's interlocutor in London on April 3, 2004 when he received the call. Benotman is himself reputed to have been a member of the LIFG's governing Shura council. According to Benotman, his unnamed colleague told him that Fakhet had called—only minutes before taking his life in a spectacular suicide operation—in order to discuss "business."[13]

It is in fact a common practice for suicide bombers to contact their "emirs," often in far-away places, before proceeding with their operations. Around seven in the morning on April 11, 2002, for example, a certain Nizar Nawar is known to have placed a call to Christian Ganczarski, asking for the "blessing" of the German Muslim convert and known bin Laden confidante. Nawar was on the Tunisian island of Djerba. Ganszarski was at home in Germany. "God willing," Ganczarski replied, ". . . God's grace and blessing be with you."[14] Shortly over one hour later, Nawar drove a truck packed with explosives into the El Ghriba synagogue, killing himself and nineteen other people.

The fact that Fakhet would have contacted a leading LIFG member just minutes before the Leganés blast not only clearly suggests that the LIFG was privy to the plans of the Madrid terror cell: it suggests that it was an LIFG leader who gave the final go-ahead for their execution. In light of the background and history of the Madrid terror plot, this would hardly be surprising.

The Spanish investigations into the train bombings provide a broader and obviously sinister context for Fakhet's contacts with LIFG members in early 2004, and they make clear that the LIFG's connection to the train plot was anything but an incidental by-product of group members' alleged interest in the "furniture business." The "business" of the LIFG was jihad.

---

13. "Las amistades libias de El Tunecino," *El País*, April 29, 2010.
14. "Osamas deutscher General," *Stern*, no. 32/2005.

According to Spanish prosecutors, in February 2002, LIFG leaders met in Istanbul with counterparts from two kindred North African organizations: the Moroccan Islamic Fighting Group and the Tunisian Islamic Fighting Group.[15] The jihadist leaders agreed that Muslims did not have to travel to active war zones in order to participate in jihad, but could do so by undertaking operations in their places of residence.

The decision would take on new significance following the American-led invasion and occupation of Iraq in 2003. In an October 18, 2003 statement broadcast on Al-Jazeera, Osama bin Laden threatened America's coalition partners, explicitly naming Spain as a target. "We reserve the right to retaliate at the appropriate time and place against all countries involved," he warned, "especially the UK, Spain, Australia, Poland, Japan, and Italy . . . ." Within six months of bin Laden's announcement, Spain would be hit. One year later, on July 7, 2005, it would be the turn of the United Kingdom, when four suicide bombers struck the London transport system killing some 52 people and wounding hundreds of others.

Spanish investigators trace back the origins of the Madrid train plot to the February 2002 meeting of the North African "fighting groups" in Istanbul. The LIFG's Moroccan counterpart, the Moroccan Islamic Fighting Group (MIFG), played an especially conspicuous role in the plot. Indeed, it was a Madrid-based MIFG operative by the name of Mustafa Maymouni who, following the Istanbul meeting, was tasked with forming a terror cell in Spain.

---

15. Prosecutor's Revised Statement of Facts ("*Calificación Definitiva*"), June 4, 2007, p. 14. The original indictment prepared by investigative judge Juan del Olmo mentions rather a February *2003* meeting in Istanbul between the Libyan and Moroccan groups and states that it was already at this time that the decision was taken to attack Spain. Del Olmo's indictment states, moreover, that the two groups were acting under the "ideological leadership of al-Qaeda" and, more specifically, of Abu Musab al-Zarqawi. Juzgado Central De Instrucción N° 6, Sumario N° 20/2004, April 10, 2006, p. 1354. There are some problems of consistency with Del Olmo's version of events: for example, as concerns the role attributed to al-Zarqawi, who did not officially join forces with bin Laden and al-Qaeda until October 2004.

By the middle of 2003, however, Maymouni was in jail in his native Morocco, where he was suspected of having formed a second terror cell: that which on May 16, 2003 carried out a series of suicide bombings in Casablanca, killing over thirty people—not counting the twelve deceased suicide bombers—and wounding more than a hundred others. Perhaps not coincidentally, one of the targets of the attacks was a Spanish restaurant named *Casa de España*, where twenty-three people were killed. Other targets included a hotel popular with Western tourists and a Jewish community center. The arrest of Maymouni left "*El Tunecino*," Fakhet, in charge of the Madrid cell.

One of the leaders of the MIFG in Europe, Hassan el-Haski, is suspected of being, along with Rabei Osman, one of the initiators of the Madrid train plot. Still another MIFG member is suspected of having chosen the date for the attacks and given the go-ahead.[16]

But the ties between the MIFG and the LIFG were extremely close: so close that by the beginning of the last decade, they appear to have been operating as, in effect, a single organization. If it was the MIFG operative Maymouni who recruited Fakhet and the other members of the Madrid terror cell, Maymouni himself was recruited in turn by a certain Amer Azizi—aka "Othman al-Andalusi"—and Azizi, though Moroccan-born, was a member of the *Libyan* Islamic Fighting Group.

The Spanish counter-terrorism expert Fernando Reinares has highlighted the key role that Azizi played in the coalescence—and perhaps indeed activation—of the Madrid train plot.[17] On Reinares's

---

16. Namely, the Belgian-based MIFG member Youssef Belhadj (apparently no relation to LIFG leader Abdul Hakim). In the 2007 Spanish "3/11" trial, both Haski and Belhadj would be found guilty of forming part of a terrorist organization. But in a ruling that parallels the court's judgment on Rabei Osman, neither would be held directly responsible for the train bombings—this despite the fact that Belhadj at least, like Osman, appears to have had foreknowledge of the attacks. The great peculiarity of the Spanish "3/11" judgment is that it, in effect, fails to attribute intellectual, as opposed to operational, responsibility for the attacks to anyone at all.

17. Fernando Reinares, "11-M: la conexión Al Qaeda," *El País*, December 17, 2009; Fernando Reinares, "The Madrid Bombings and Global Jihadism," *Survival*, vol.

count, Azizi is mentioned in at least 141 of the 240 volumes comprising the complete judicial investigation of the plot.

Azizi had already been named as a co-conspirator in a 2003 Spanish indictment against presumptive members of the al-Qaeda network in Spain. According to Spanish investigators, al-Qaeda operatives in Spain—including Amer Azizi—had connections to the Hamburg Cell that planned the 9/11 attacks. In July 2001, 9/11 plot leader and later suicide pilot Mohammed Atta is known to have met with fellow Hamburg cell member Ramzi bin al-Shibh in Tarragona, Spain. Members of the Spanish al-Qaeda cell are supposed to have facilitated the meeting.

A warrant for Azizi's arrest was issued just two months after the 9/11 attacks, on November 12, 2001. Azizi was, however, out of the country at the time. Despite apparently returning to Spain shortly thereafter, he managed to avoid arrest and abscond to Pakistan.[18]

Not surprisingly, many figures who already appeared in the earlier Spanish al-Qaeda investigation would re-emerge as key figures in the Madrid train plot. Azizi's specific involvement with the train plot cell did not end with his recruitment of Maymouni. According to Reinares, citing the official Spanish documentation, Azizi was also a "friend" of Fakhet with whom he maintained "frequent contacts" by e-mail even after fleeing Spain.[19] He also had close ties to other cell members.

As Reinares relates, Azizi received jihadist training at the "Martyr Abu Yahya" camp: one of the jihadist facilities run by the LIFG in Afghanistan in the years immediately preceding 9/11. In May 1997, five years prior to the fateful 2002 meeting in Istanbul, the LIFG and MIFG had already convened a series of meetings in Turkey in order to coordinate their activities. It was agreed that the LIFG would "host

---

52, no. 2, April-May 2010; and Fernando Reinares, "The Evidence of Al-Qa`ida's Role in the 2004 Madrid Attack," *CTC Sentinal* (Combating Terrorism Center at West Point), vol. 5 issue 3, March 2012.

18. Reinares, "The Evidence of Al-Qa`ida's Role in the 2004 Madrid Attack," note 12.

19. Reinares, "The Madrid Bombings and Global Jihadism."

weapons training and jihad indoctrination" for Moroccans at LIFG camps in Afghanistan.[20] According to Moroccan court records, the LIFG was represented at the meetings by, among others, Shura council member Abdul Rahman al-Faqih and commander Abu-Abdallah al-Sadiq—i.e. Abdul Hakim Belhadj.[21] Amer Azizi was one of the Moroccan beneficiaries of the agreed arrangement.

Instead of merely receiving training at "Martyr Abu Yahya," however, Azizi became a full-fledged member of the Libyan group. As Reinares shows, he would go on to rise to the very upper echelons of al-Qaeda as such. He was reportedly killed by an American hellfire missile in North Waziristan, not far from the Pakistani-Afghan border, in December 2005. Also reportedly killed in the attack was none other than Hamza Rabia: the head of al-Qaeda's "external operations." Rabia had succeeded 9/11 "mastermind" Khalid Sheikh Mohammed in the post following Mohammed's arrest in Pakistan in March 2003.

In the nomenclature employed by al-Qaeda at the time, "external operations" referred to terror attacks outside of the organization's "home" base in Afghanistan and the tribal zones of Pakistan. A biography of Azizi from jihadist websites identifies him as Rabia's lieutenant and alludes to his role in preparing "external" terror attacks on Western targets. As his biographer put it, Azizi helped to prepare "the lions that came from far away . . . to transform the tranquility of the crusaders into a hell."[22]

Azizi's association with Hamza Rabia does not only illustrate the intertwining of the LIFG and al-Qaeda hierarchies. It also suggests that the decision to proceed with the Madrid attacks came directly from the al-Qaeda leadership—on Reinares's account, via Amer Azizi.

---

20. US Treasury Department, "Treasury Designates UK-Based Individuals, Entities Financing Al Qaida-Affiliated LIFG," February 8, 2006. See too UN Security Council 1267 Committee, Narrative Summary of Reasons for Listing: Abd Al-Rahman Al-Faqih.

21. Cited in Kohlmann, "Dossier: Libyan Islamic Fighting Group (LIFG)," p. 15.

22. Cited in Reinares, "The Evidence of Al-Qa`ida's Role in the 2004 Madrid Attack."

While at "Martyr Abu Yahya," presumably in the year 2000, Azizi got to know another LIFG recruit by the name of Abdulatif Mourafik, aka "Malek al-Andalusi."[23] According to Reinares, citing confidential Spanish police intelligence reports, it was the LIFG operative Mourafik who instructed Maymouni to form both the Madrid terror cell and a terror cell in Kenitra in his native Morocco. Like Maymouni, Mourafik would be convicted by a Moroccan court of complicity in the May 2003 Casablanca bombings.

Although, unlike Azizi, he was not charged as a co-conspirator in the 2003 Spanish al-Qaeda indictment, Mourafik's name also comes up in the indictment. By mid-2001, Amer Azizi had completed his jihadist training in Afghanistan and returned to Spain. His old friend from "Martyr Abu Yahya," Abdulatif Mourafik, was apparently having trouble getting hold of him. According to the indictment, on July 31, 2001, Mourafik placed a call to Imad Eddin Barakat Yarkas, aka "Abu Dahdah," the head of the local al-Qaeda network in Spain. Mourafik explained that he had been trying to call Azizi for two weeks without success, and he asked Yarkas for Azizi's current number.

Before getting off the phone, Mourafik sent Yarkas greetings from a certain "Abu al Munzer," i.e. "Abu al-Munthir," i.e. none other than LIFG chief ideologue Abu al-Munthir al-Saadi.[24] The Spanish indictment indicates that Mourafik placed his call to Yarkas from an unnamed foreign country. Mourafik, however, is known to have still been in Afghanistan in the summer of 2001. By his own admission,

---

23. According to Mourafik's own testimony, he first arrived in Afghanistan in May 2000. Juzgado Central De Instrucción N° 6, Sumario N° 20/2004, April 10, 2006, p. 1240. As mentioned above, Azizi himself went by the alias "Othman al-Andalusi." Al-Qaeda members frequently use place-names in their aliases. The use by Mourafik and Azizi of the alias "al-Andalusi"—"the Andalusian"—indicates a connection to Spain. At the height of Islamic domination of the Iberian Peninsula in the middle Ages, the Islamic state of al-Andalus comprised not only modern day Andalusia but the virtual entirety of modern day Spain. Questioned by investigators, Mourafik claimed, somewhat implausibly, to have been called "al-Andalusi" because of the proximity of Morocco to Andalusia.

24. Juzgado Central De Instruccion N° 005, Sumario (Proc.Ordinario) 0000035/2001, September 17, 2003, pp. 109, 254, 597.

on September 9th of that year, two days before the 9/11 attacks, he dined with al-Munthir in Kabul.[25]

Like Amer Azizi, Mourafik appears to have been a Moroccan-born LIFG recruit. But a leading Libyan member of the LIFG has also been connected to the Casablanca bombings: namely, Abdul Rahman al-Faqih, the LIFG Shura Council member who attended the LIFG-MIFG consultations in Turkey in 1997. Al-Faqih was convicted in absentia by a Moroccan court for his alleged role in the attacks.[26] We will have occasion to meet him again later on in our story. The Spanish "3-11" indictment, which highlights the interconnections between the Casablanca and Madrid plots, states that the planning of the Casablanca attacks was jointly undertaken by "various leaders" of both the Moroccan and Libyan organizations.[27]

But the ties between the MIFG and the LIFG were not only operational. They were also familial—or, more precisely, family ties appear to have been created between the two groups for operational purposes. Thus Fakhet, the head of the Madrid terror cell, Maymouni, the MIFG operative who assembled the cell, and al-Hashim, the Belhadj associate and LIFG "communicator" in London, were all brothers-in-law. Fakhet and al-Hashim were married to sisters of Maymouni. According to Spanish intelligence, Maymouni married off his sisters to the two men on the instructions of Mourafik, the same Mourafik who is likewise supposed to have instructed him to form the Madrid cell and the Kenitra terror cell in Morocco.[28]

Commenting on al-Hashim's family ties to Fakhet and Maymouni, the UK's Special Immigration Appeals Commission dryly noted that

25. See United States Department of Justice, In the Matter of Mourad El Hamyani, DHS Brief in Support of Appeal, April 29, 2008, p. 31.

26. US Treasury Department, "Treasury Designates UK-Based Individuals, Entities Financing Al Qaida-Affiliated LIFG," February 8, 2006; UN Security Council 1267 Committee, Narrative Summary of Reasons for Listing: Abd Al-Rahman Al-Faqih.

27. Juzgado Central De Instrucción N° 6, Sumario N° 20/2004, April 10, 2006, p. 546.

28. *ABC* (Spanish daily), August 1, 2005.

the British Home Office "attributed considerable weight to these familial connections, and sees them as rather more than unhappy coincidences." The court concluded that al-Hashim's "links to Maymouni and Fakhet are not mere misfortune or coincidence; we believe from experience that such family relationships with like-minded people add to contacts, cover, and security."[29]

The recruiter of the Madrid terror cell, Mustafa Maymouni, appears, moreover, to be related by marriage to yet another leading member of the LIFG: none other than LIFG chief Abdul-Hakim Belhadj. According to Spanish intelligence, Belhadj is married to a cousin of Maymouni.[30]

It is surely no accident that Abdul-Hakim Belhadj's role in the Libyan rebellion only became public *after* his forces had taken control of his native Tripoli in late August 2011. The conquest of Tripoli was essentially the work of NATO bombing, which had destroyed the city's defenses and both literally and figuratively reduced the command centers of the old regime to rubble. Belhadj and his men merely had to move in and pick up the pieces. It would undoubtedly have lessened the enthusiasm of the Western public for the NATO air campaign, if it had come out that NATO bombing was paving the way for a known bin Laden associate to take control of the Libyan capital.

Since then, it has become common to read in the American press that the LIFG, despite its long history of closeness to al-Qaeda, was merely a patriotic organization dedicated to overturning the Qaddafi regime in Libya. By virtue of sheer mind-numbing repetition, the claim has perhaps lost some of its inherent implausibility in the

---

29. Special Immigration Appeals Commission judgment of April 27, 2007, Appeal No: SC/42 and 50/2005, paragraphs 62 and 73. In the aftermath of the Casablanca and Madrid attacks, the usefulness of the family ties at providing cover will obviously have been diminished. Thus, in speaking with British investigators, al-Hashim appears to have avoided mentioning his family connection to Fakhet—undoubtedly, fearing that it would raise suspicions more readily than dissipate them. According to the immigration court ruling, al-Hashim claimed to have met his wife "through an Arabic Muslim website" (paragraph 62).

30. *ABC* (Spanish daily), August 1, 2005.

eyes of the American public. Spaniards, on the other hand, will be less easily convinced. The numerous connections of the LIFG to the Madrid train plot make abundantly clear that the LIFG was heavily involved in global jihad and even decisively so in the "external," strictly terrorist, component of al-Qaeda's operations.

Moreover, the LIFG's involvement in the realization of Osama bin Laden's grand strategy to punish America's allies appears not to have been limited to the Madrid train bombings. As will be seen in chapter 9, there is evidence that yet another LIFG leader, no less an authority than Abu al-Munthir al-Saadi, helped to inspire and guide the young British Muslims who would bring the frontlines of jihad to the streets of London one year later.

CHAPTER 6

The Al-Qaeda Veterans/Rebel Commanders

The outing of Abdul-Hakim Belhadj as the commander of the rebel forces in Tripoli provided spectacular confirmation of the involvement of the Libyan branch of al-Qaeda in the anti-Qaddafi rebellion—so spectacular that not even the mainstream American media could entirely ignore it. But Belhadj is by no means the only known al-Qaeda-linked militant to have played a major role in the rebellion. Already at the outset of the unrest in eastern Libya, a Libyan government official was reported to have told European diplomats that the uprising in Derna was being led by a former Guantánamo detainee by the name of Abdul-Karim al-Hasadi. The claim was greeted with derision by American commentators—despite the evidence of the Sinjar records and despite Libya's recent record of close cooperation with US counterterrorism efforts.

As it turns out, the report was indeed mistaken: Not one, but rather *two* known al-Qaeda-linked militants were playing leading roles in the rebellion in Derna. There was a former Guantánamo inmate involved. His name, however, was not al Abdul-Karim al-Hasadi, but rather Abu Sufian bin Qumu. Bin Qumu was transferred to Guantánamo in May 2002. He had fled Afghanistan in late 2001, after having fought with the Taliban, and he was initially detained by Pakistani security forces in Peshawar. Prior to that, he had been a longtime associate of Osama bin Laden in both Afghanistan and Sudan. A leaked Department of Defense detainee assessment contains a long list of bin Qumu's terrorist contacts, including both Belhadj and al-Munthir.[1] The assessment notes, furthermore, that a document belonging to 9/11 financier Mustafa al-Hawsawi identifies bin Qumu as "an Al-Qaida member receiving family support."

Bin Qumu reportedly served as a trainer of rebel forces in Derna. Like the detainee assessments of the many other Guantánamo detainees who were at one time or another associated with the Libyan Islamic Fighting Group, the bin Qumu assessment also includes a brief analytical note about the LIFG. Especially in light of the recent revisionism in the American media regarding the nature and scope of the LIFG's aims, the note is worth citing here. It identifies the LIFG as a "tier 1 counterterrorism target" and defines "tier 1 targets" as terror groups that "have demonstrated the intention and the capability to attack US persons or interests."

Unlike bin Qumu, the local rebel commander al-Hasadi had never been sent to Guantánamo. Like both bin Qumu and Belhadj, however, he had indeed been detained by American authorities. Al-Hasadi's first name is sometimes given as "Abdul-Karim," as per the original information provided by the then Libyan authorities, and sometimes as "Abdul-Hakim." According to his own admissions in a March 2011 interview with the Italian newspaper *Il Sole 24 Ore*, after fighting against coalition forces in Afghanistan, he was detained in Peshawar in 2002 and turned over to American custody. After being held for several months, he was then transferred to Libya, where he

---

1. See JTF GTMO Detainee Assessment: Abu Sufian Ibrahim Ahmed Hamouda (aka Abu Sufian bin Qumu), April 22, 2005.

would continue to be detained for several years by Libyan authorities.[2] He was released in 2008, apparently as part of the same amnesty program for LIFG members to which Belhadj would owe his release two years later.

In the same interview, al-Hasadi likewise admitted to having personally recruited "around 25" Libyans to join al-Qaeda in Iraq. Some of his recruits, he added, had since returned to Libya and were fighting against Libyan army forces on the frontlines in Ajdabiya, a strategic town some 90 miles due south of Benghazi on the coastal road that connects Benghazi to Tripoli in the west. The battle would undoubtedly have been easier than the battles that al-Hasadi's forces had experienced in Iraq—thanks, namely, to the NATO air support they enjoyed. Al-Hasadi's interview with *Il Sole 24 Ore* appeared on March 22. Within days, massive NATO airstrikes would force the Libyan army to retreat from Ajdabiya, allowing rebel forces to move in unopposed.

A few weeks later, the Libyan army had again advanced on Ajdabiya, sending rebel forces fleeing. Only yet another massive demonstration of NATO air power changed the tide in the rebels' favor. Asked by a French reporter about the aid he was receiving from his erstwhile enemies, al-Hasadi responded with unconcealed contempt, "Someone who is drowning will reach out to anyone, even the devil."[3]

In speaking with Sara Daniel from the weekly *Le Nouvel Observateur*, Al-Hasadi was no less open about his jihadist résumé and convictions than he had been when speaking to *Il Sole 24 Ore*. "What's surprising when one speaks with al-Hasadi," Daniel wrote about her encounter with him in Derna, "is the almost brutal frankness with which he embraces his hatred of the West and his religious extremism." Referring to his Afghan period, al-Hasadi told Daniel, "I'd be lying to you if I said that I did not meet some of the great heroes of

---

2. *Il Sole 24 Ore*, March 22, 2011.
3. Sara Daniel, "Avec les djihadistes de Derna," *Le Nouvel Observateur* (online), April 14, 2011.

the *Ummah*. I was never lucky enough to fight alongside Osama bin Laden, but I often spent time with Ayman al-Zawahiri."

According to Daniel, after being turned over to American custody by the Pakistanis in 2002, al-Hasadi would eventually end up being detained at the Bagram Air Base near Kabul. Although less well known in the West than the Guantánamo facility, detention at Bagram was a rite of passage for numerous high-profile al-Qaeda members and affiliated fighters, and it is equally as famous in jihadist lore.[4]

In American news reports, al-Hasadi was commonly depicted as the rebel military commander responsible for the "defense" of Derna. The description is obviously bogus, given that Derna lies some 150 miles to the east of Benghazi and hence was well behind the front lines for the entirety of the Libyan conflict. Numerous European news reports, like that of Sara Daniel, make clear that in reality Derna was rather the staging area for *offensive* operations conducted under al-Hasadi's leadership.

It should be noted that the American public's awareness of the extent of the involvement of prominent al-Qaeda-linked militants in the Libyan rebellion was artificially limited as a result of some influential misreporting on the part of the *New York Times*. In an August 2011 report from Tripoli highlighting the role of Belhadj, the *Times* erroneously claimed that Belhadj was "also known as" Abdul-Hakim al-Hasadi.[5] The *Times* would go on quietly to correct the error,[6] but only after a full two weeks had passed. Both the error and the delay in its rectification are somewhat curious, given that the *Times* had had a face-to-face sit-down with al-Hasadi the previous March.[7]

In a further curious twist, after Belhadj's emergence in August 2011 as the head of Tripoli's military council, al-Hasadi dropped out

---

4. Given both the plethora of aliases used by LIFG member and the plethora of transliterations used in official documents in rendering Arabic names, it is unclear under what name al-Hasadi was known to American officials.

5. *New York Times*, August 30, 2011.

6. *New York Times*, September 13, 2011.

7. *New York Times*, March 7, 2011.

of the Western news altogether for many months, as if he had indeed never existed. Nonetheless, last spring, Sherif Elhelwa, an Egyptian correspondent for the alternative youth-oriented website *Vice*, had no trouble tracking him down at home in his native Derna, and he was as voluble as ever—if, albeit, a bit more evasive.[8]

Having made him disappear in summer 2011, after the fall of Tripoli, the *New York Times* finally rediscovered al-Hasadi the following June—now, however, reinvented as a moderate Muslim dedicated to "peaceful change" via the ballot box.[9] This would be reassuring, if it were not for the fact that the *New York Times* had already presented al-Hasadi as a moderate when first meeting him in March 2011.

In particular, pace reports that he had proclaimed a local Islamic emirate, the *Times* cited al-Hasadi as saying that he had no interest in establishing an Islamic state in Libya. This was at roughly the same time that al-Hasadi was proudly telling European reporters that he had fought alongside the Taliban in Afghanistan, considered Osama bin Laden and Ayman al-Zawahiri as "heroes," personally knew the latter, recruited fighters for al-Qaeda in Iraq . . ., *and* was now aiming "to cut Qaddafi's throat *and establish an Islamic state in Libya.*"[10] Virtually alone among the world's press, the *New York Times* somehow managed to miss al-Hasadi's "brutal frankness."

Belhadj, bin Qumu and al-Hasadi are all al-Qaeda-linked jihadist veterans who were known to American officials before the outbreak of the conflict in Libya. But numerous other lesser-known veterans of jihad undoubtedly participated in the anti-Qaddafi rebellion as well.

---

8. For Elhelwa's interview with al-Hasadi, see part 3 of his April 2012 *Vice* documentary "Waiting for al-Qaeda."

9. *New York Times*, June 23, 2012. The *Times* also continued to whitewash al-Hasadi's jihadist past. Despite al-Hasadi's serial admissions of his having fought in Afghanistan, per the *New York Times*, he merely went to Afghanistan in order to "study under the Taliban."

10. "En Libye, les djihadistes montent au front," *Le Journal du Dimanche*, April 2, 2011. The article identifies the source for the quote as a rebel commander from Derna named "Hakim al-Sadi." But it is clear from the context and from biographical details that the commander in question is in fact Abdul-Hakim al-Hasadi.

Al-Hasadi himself admitted this, in noting the presence of al-Qaeda in Iraq recruits among his Libyan fighters. Similarly, as we saw in chapter 4, Belhadj's lieutenants have made no secret of their experience training and fighting in Afghanistan.

Some of these hitherto lesser lights of global jihad have even gone on to make a name for themselves precisely in the Libya war—if not in the West, at least locally and in Arabic-language jihadist media. One such rising star is none other than Wisam bin Hamid, the commander of the rebel forces at Sirte whose units we came across in chapter 3 flying the black flags of jihad. As noted above, bin Hamid has been reported to be thirty-five years old, and from the many videos of him available on local pro-rebellion Libyan websites he looks indeed to be in his mid-thirties. Despite his relative youth, however, he appears to be no newcomer to jihad.

On October 29, 2011—nine days after bin Hamid's men slaughtered Muammar al-Qaddafi outside of Sirte and not yet a week after Mustafa Abdul Jalil proclaimed the "liberation" of Libya—a glowing portrait of bin Hamid and his troops appeared on the Islamist Internet forum *Al-Fetn* (alfetn.com).[11] According to the *Al-Fetn* text, before becoming a commander of "the *mujahideen* who fought al-Qaddafi's battalions" in Libya, bin Hamid "waged holy war in Afghanistan and from there went to Iraq." If this is correct, then it means that on no less than three of the key fronts in the Libyan war, NATO partnered with rebel commanders who had previously collaborated with al-Qaeda in Afghanistan and/or Iraq: al-Hasadi on the Eastern front, Belhadj in Tripoli, and bin Hamid during the siege of Sirte.

The *Al-Fetn* text is accompanied by a photo that is said to show one of bin Hamid's lieutenants. The heavily-armed *mujahid* sports long hair and a thick beard and wears a long Afghan tunic over his

---

11. The name of the forum, *Al Fetn*, is the plural of the Arabic word *fitna*, meaning "strife" or "troubles." The term typically has millenarian connotations in Islamist usage. The cited text is consultable at http://alfetn.com/vb3/showthread.php?t=57785.

army fatigues. He strides down the road surrounded by clean-shaven and somewhat bemused-looking Libyans in jeans and sneakers. "I swear by God that I stood a weakling in front of this photograph when I saw the men of the state of the Caliphate," the author of the *Al-Fetn* text exults.

"I stood a weakling in front of the men of the Caliphate"

In ecstatic religious prose, bin Hamid's chronicler celebrates the victory over Qaddafi and the itinerary followed by bin Hamid and the *mujahideen* in leading up to it:

From the East in the country of the Afghans to the Country of the Two Rivers [Iraq] travelling to the land of Libya, we have approached the North and, by the grace and strength of God, we have seized the reins to determine the bloody battle.

The *Al-Fetn* text also records that a gathering of the *mujahideen*—"with weapons and equipment"—took place in Benghazi's "Freedom Square" on October 26th, i.e. three days after NTC chair Mustafa Abdul Jalil proclaimed Libya's "liberation" at the same spot. The assembled fighters issued a declaration announcing the formation of a "supreme board of the *mujahideen*" under the leadership of "Sheikh Wisam bin Hamid." The declaration goes on to cite bin Hamid's emphatic statement that "The Islamic *sharia* is a red line, we will not cede one rule of it, and Islam is the only law-giver and not [merely] the foundation [of the law]."

The declaration of the supreme board of the Libyan *mujahideen* likewise contained two further programmatic points that are worth noting: firstly, that the *mujahideen* would continue "the purging of Libya from followers of false idols [*tawaghit*] whoever they are," and, secondly, that "the *mujahideen* will not hand over their weapons to anyone, but will remain a force to protect Libyans from foreign machinations."

In accordance with *Takfiri* doctrine, "followers of false idols" has to be understood very largely to include not only non-Muslims, but also—or perhaps indeed *especially*—Muslims whose practices are regarded as heterodox and "impure." In the present context, it would also clearly include followers of Qaddafi. The term *tawaghit* is extended in contemporary Islamist usage to Arab leaders (Qaddafi, Mubarak, Assad, etc.) who represent "false idols" inasmuch as they fail to rule according to the precepts of Islam.

The two points help to explain much that has occurred in Libya since its "liberation" by NATO and the *mujahideen*, from the the highly publicized March 2012 desecration of the Commonwealth war cemetery in Benghazi to the persecution and killing of real or perceived supporters of the *ancien régime* to the serial destruction of Sufi monuments and mausoleums. As documented in amateur video of the incident, the attack on the Commonwealth war cemetery would culminate in the ritual demolition of a commemorative Christian cross. The adherents of al-Qaeda and kindred Islamic fundamentalist groups regard shrines to Sufi "saints" as likewise idolatrous and un-Islamic.

Wisam bin Hamid's stated determination to protect Libya against "foreign machinations" by force of arms is of particular significance to an, in the meanwhile, even more notorious episode: namely, the September 11, 2012 attacks in Benghazi that left American ambassador to Libya Chris Stevens and three other Americans dead. The attacks form part of a series of attacks on Western diplomatic targets that have taken place in Benghazi since Libya's "liberation."

According to several concordant reports, a contingent of American marines that was dispatched from Tripoli on the night of the anti-American attacks was met in Benghazi by a Libyan security escort provided by none other than Wisam bin Hamid's Libya Shield Brigade.[12] It was this escort that would accompany the marines to the supposedly secret "safe house" in which American personnel took refuge following the initial assault on the American diplomatic mission in which Ambassador Stevens and a mission employee were killed. The "safe house," however, turned out to be neither secret nor safe. After the arrival of the American marines, the "safe house" would be the target of a second attack in which two more Americans died.

---

12. See, for instance, "Libya rescue squad ran into fierce, accurate ambush," Reuters, September 12, 2012 and "After Attack in Libya, Ambush Struck Rescuers," *New York Times*, September 20, 2012. A more detailed account of the Libya Shield Brigade's alleged role in "protecting" Americans is provided by the French daily *Le Figaro* in "Benghazi: le recit de l'assaut anti-américain," *Le Figaro*, September 17, 2012. The *Le Figaro* account is based upon interviews with members of the brigade, including Keis bin Hamid, the brother of Wisam bin Hamid.

In the Western news media, the 9/11 Benghazi attacks have frequently been attributed to an al-Qaeda-linked radical Islamic militia going by the name Ansar al-Sharia. Proof of Ansar al-Sharia responsibility is said to include witness reports of the attackers waving, as the *New York Times* has put it, "the black flag favored by such ultraconservative jihadis."[13] On the other hand, the members of the Libya Shield detachment presumably figure among the Libyans whom the Obama administration has praised for "fighting side by side" American forces on the night of the attacks.[14]

This is to say that in the through-the-looking-glass world presented as reality by Western media and the American government, an attack by Islamic extremists on American diplomatic personnel is supposed to have been beaten back by an Islamist brigade that flaunts its allegiance to precisely the same ideology as the alleged assailants: the ideology, that is to say, of al-Qaeda. In a more rational universe, one would have to suppose rather that elements of Libya Shield were in on the plot to attack the mission and that the brigade "escort" alerted the attackers to the location of the "safe house."[15]

The black flags favored by Ansar al-Sharia are the same black flags favored by Wisam bin Hamid's troops. Indeed, there is strong reason to believe that Ansar al-Sharia is not so much a distinct militia as a movement cutting across virtually all the Eastern Libya militias, including Libya Shield. In the strict sense of the term, they are all Ansar al-Sharia, i.e. "supporters of the sharia." The June 6, 2012

---

13. "U.S. May Have Put Mistaken Faith in Libya Site's Security," *New York Times*, September 30, 2012.

14. The exact expression comes from American Ambassador to the U.N. Susan Rice. But both President Obama and Secretary of State Hillary Clinton made similar remarks.

15. Whatever the US administration may have said about the supposed solidarity of its Libyan "allies," Wisam bin Hamid himself did little to hide his true feelings about the American casualties. Alluding to the bogus reports according to which the attacks were sparked by a blasphemous American film about Mohammed, bin Hamid told Reuters, "The deaths and injuries and attacks are all nothing compared to insulting the Prophet." Cited in "In Libya, deadly fury took US envoys by surprise," Reuters, September 12, 2012. Reuters misspells bin Hamid's name as "Wissam Buhmeid."

Benghazi rally "in support of the sharia" makes this clear. (See chapter 3.) Libya Shield was not only present at the rally. It was in fact one of the sponsoring organizations. The Libya Shield logo is clearly visible on advance publicity materials for the rally – right next to the logo of Ansar al-Sharia. Moreover, Wisam bin Hamid's October 26, 2011 declaration on behalf of the supreme board of the Libyan *mujahideen* already set the tone: "The Islamic *sharia* is a red line, we will not cede one rule of it...."

Poster announcing June 6, 2012 Rally in Support of the Sharia in Benghazi. Note logos of Libya Shield and Ansar al-Sharia (4th and 3rd from right)

If members of Libya Shield were in on the 9/11 Benghazi attacks, incidentally, they could have benefitted from insider knowledge that members of less influential Libyan militias surely lacked. An unclassified diplomatic cable, which was signed by Ambassador Stevens on the very day of his death, shows that only two days before the attacks American officials in Benghazi met with none other than Libya Shield commander Wisam bin Hamid.[16]

---

16. The cable misspells Bin Hamid's last name as "bin Ahmed." See American Embassy Tripoli, Benghazi Weekly Report, September 11, 2002, paragraph 4. The cable was released by the House Oversight Committee in the aftermath of the Benghazi attacks. It is consultable at http://oversight.house.gov/wp-content/uploads/2012/10/9-11-12-Memo.pdf.

CHAPTER 7

Qaddafi, the "Apostate"

Few if any Westerners will have heard of the declaration of Wisam bin Hamid and his supreme board of the Libyan *mujahideen*. But in his speech in Benghazi three days earlier, NTC chair Mustafa Abdul Jalil already anticipated the demands of the *mujahideen*, announcing, at the same time as he proclaimed Libya's "liberation," that all Libyan laws contradicting the *sharia* were henceforth null and void. He made a point of specifically declaring the abrogation of the progressive Qaddafi-era marriage law, which restricted polygamy and significantly upgraded women's rights in matters of marriage and divorce in general.[1]

Abdul Jalil's announcement came as a surprise for Western observers. Given that he wears the sign of his piety on his forehead in the form of the darkened "prayer bump" or *zabibah* created through vigorous prostration during prayer, it probably should not have.

---

1. The Qaddafi-era legislation did not quite ban polygamy, but in most circumstances it effectively did so—namely, by making women the arbiters of whether their husbands could marry additional wives!

Western observers had always been determined to see the anti-Qaddafi rebellion as a "democracy movement." In a remarkable feat of solipsism, they found confirmation for their preconceptions in English-language NTC statements replete with high-sounding boilerplate that had undoubtedly been composed with the aid of western advisors or PR agencies. But one did not need to wait for the rebellion to triumph in order to recognize its Islamist inspiration. From the very start, clear evidence was available that the most fervent opponents of Qaddafi rejected his rule not as undemocratic, but above all, as *un-Islamic*.

The February 17th "Day of Rage" was sponsored by a London-based organization named the National Conference for the Libyan Opposition (NCLO). It should be noted that numerous LIFG members are known to have taken refuge in the United Kingdom. They include, for instance, none other than Ziyad al-Hashim: the LIFG "propagandist" and website creator whom we met in chapter 5 taking "business" calls in London from Serhane ben Abdelmajid Fakhet, the leader of the terror cell that perpetrated the Madrid train bombings.

On February 15—just two days before the scheduled "Day of Rage" and the very day on which the first signs of unrest appeared in Libya—the NCLO posted an Arabic-language article on its website titled "Qaddafi: Islam's Enemy no. 1."[2] The text amounts to an indictment of Qaddafi for a long list of alleged crimes against Islamic orthodoxy. The latter include his discouraging women from wearing the traditional Islamic "veil," his proposal that Jews and Christians should be allowed to visit Mecca, and his suggestion that the Quran might not be "suitable for the age." In keeping with the list of charges, a popular video clip on pro-rebellion websites and YouTube pages shows Qaddafi nonchalantly removing a women's facial covering or "*niqab*."[3]

---

2. For an English translation, see "'Gaddafi: Islam's Enemy no. 1': A document from the Libyan opposition," *Pajamas Media*, April 1, 2011.
3. The clip can be viewed, for instance, at http://www.youtube.com/watch?v=KByzUah5YzA.

But of all the crimes included in the NCLO list, the greatest crime committed by Qaddafi in the eyes of his Islamist critics was undoubtedly his outright rejection of the *sunna*. The *sunna* are the traditional Islamic practices that derive from the accounts of Mohammed's acts and teachings known as the *hadith*. The term "Sunni Islam" refers to the *sunna*, and the *sunna* are at the core of the ultra-orthodox interpretation of Islam defended by al-Qaeda and kindred fundamentalist movements. It is hardly surprising that an Arab leader who rejects the *sunna* would be regarded as a very great heretic indeed.

The NCLO text ends with a rhetorical question: "Have you heard of any tyrant who has done to Islam and its people what the criminal Qaddafi has done?"

The tenor of the document echoes that of the November 2007 announcement of the LIFG's incorporation into al-Qaeda (see chapter 4)—albeit the al-Qaeda statement places greater emphasis on geo-political considerations. Indeed, in his recorded message Ayman al-Zawahiri likewise describes Qaddafi as an "enemy of Islam." More precisely, al-Zawahiri refers to the confrontation with "the enemies of Islam, al-Qaddafi and his masters the Crusaders of Washington." Ironically, in light of subsequent developments, the official fusion of the LIFG and al-Qaeda appears at least in part to have been motivated by Qaddafi's counter-terrorism cooperation with the United States.

Al-Zawahiri was joined on the recording by Abu Laith al-Libi: an Afghan theater al-Qaeda military commander who came to al-Qaeda from the LIFG. Several leading figures in al-Qaeda have used the pseudonym "al-Libi": "The Libyan." Abu Laith al-Libi was reportedly killed in an American airstrike just two months after the release of his joint message with al-Zawahiri.

In his contribution to the recording, al-Libi repeatedly describes Qaddafi as an "apostate" and his rule as "an apostate regime." "It is with the grace of God that we were hoisting the banner of jihad against this apostate regime under the leadership of the Libyan Islamic Fighting

Group," he explains. He encourages Libyans to be prepared to engage in a "new round" of jihad: "not only against the apostate al-Qaddafi's regime, but against his keepers and masters the Americans and their brothers, the infidels of the West."[4]

A particular sore spot for Qaddafi's opponents was what they perceived as his efforts to depict himself as a "prophet," and hence as on par with Mohammed. A German-language website of the Misrata-based rebel organization Wefaq Libya has posted a video clip of a long harangue from an outraged Tripoli resident taking Qaddafi to task for this act of hubris. "You dog! You Jew!" the man screams, before offering "proof" that Qaddafi could not be a prophet (namely, because he has been seen swatting flies and a prophet would not attract flies).[5]

In 2006, the Combating Terrorism Center at West Point published a detailed study of jihadist ideological sources, the *Militant Ideology Atlas*. The West Point analysts found that the tenth most popular text in the online jihadist library Tawhed.ws was a treatise on the subject of Qaddafi's "false prophecy." The text, by one Abdel Rahman Hasan, is titled *Al-Qaddafi: the Musaylima of the Era*. As the West Point analysts explain, "Musaylima, also known by the name of Haroun, is the man who sent a letter to Prophet Muhammad claiming prophethood."

The text, furthermore, "accuses Qadhdhafi of hating Islam, disrespecting the Prophet, misinterpreting the Qur'an, separating religion from the state, and separating the public and private sphere in Libyan society."[6] Those still convinced that the wellsprings of the Libyan opposition were essentially democratic in nature—or, for that matter, convinced of the compatibility of democracy and Islamism—should take particular note of the last two items in this list. The preface

---

4. An identical full English translation of both al-Zawahiri's and al-Libi's remarks is available on several websites and in Laura Mansfield's *Al-Qaeda 2007 Yearbook*. It appears to be derived from English sub-titles prepared by the al-Qaeda "media arm" as-Sahab.

5. The video is viewable at http://www.youtube.com/watch?v=_hGSjAnfhe4.

6. *Militant Ideology Atlas* (Combating Terrorism Center at West Point, November 2006), p. 78.

to *Al-Qaddafi: the Musaylima of the Era* was written by LIFG chief ideologue Abu al-Munthir.

The same fervency and the same motives that are evident in the Arabic-language texts of Qaddafi's opponents were also manifest on the front lines in the Libyan war. In early October, the Algerian newspaper *Echorouk* published a report on the siege of Sirte. The report revealed that one of the rebel battalions was led by a veteran jihadist going by the name of Abu Bilal al-Afghani: "Abu Bilal, the Afghani." "I am Libyan-born," the rebel commander said, explaining his reasons for participating in the war against Qaddafi, "and I work with my brothers in jihad against he who insulted Allah and His Messenger and denied the Sunna of his Messenger."[7]

In July, the Misrata-based rebel organization Wefaq Libya posted a video showing a group of rebels, weapons in hand, singing a jihadist anthem or "*nasheed*," in which they pledge "to bring back the purity of Islam to Tripoli." "We will take up our fight with them," the men sing:

> We will go in groups to stop them.
> We will bring back the purity of Islam to Tripoli,
> After all our humiliations, after all our humiliations.[8]

The song is known as the "*Sanakhudu Nasheed*." The corresponding line in the original version runs instead, "We will bring back the purity of Islam to al-Quds," i.e. Jerusalem.

---

7. *Echorouk*, October 11, 2011. Translated excerpts from the *Echorouk* report are available on the Roads to Iraq blog. See "Libya, exposing Al-Qaeda NATO-Jihadists in Sirte," Roads to Iraq, October 12, 2011. My thanks to the proprietor of Roads to Iraq for translating the additional passage cited above.

8. For the original video, consisting of a compilation of clips, see http://www.youtube.com/watch?v=m7qoIqd4OZo. I have translated the text from German sub-titles provided by Wefaq Libya German at http://www.youtube.com/watch?v=B8R9q9IZYH0.

CHAPTER 8

Video and Terror

Since the very first weeks of the Libyan rebellion, harrowing videos documenting rebel atrocities were readily available on the Internet. Like the graphic videos of Muammar al-Qaddafi's last moments following his capture at Sirte, the earlier atrocity videos appear, as a rule, to have been originally posted by rebel forces or rebel sympathizers themselves. Indeed, some such videos are even available on the English-language websites that served as the showcase of the rebellion to the rest of the world.[1]

In keeping with rumors of the use of sub-Saharan African mercenaries to put down the rebellion, the targets of the abuse depicted

---

1.   See, for instance, the video titled "Mercenaries who slaughtered civilians" on the Feb17 Images website: http://www.feb17images.com/mercenaries-who-slaughtered-civilians-0. The clip does not show slaughtered civilians, but rather two alleged mercenaries, both of whom are badly wounded and one of whom has clearly been repeatedly hacked with a machete. Lest there be any doubt about the origins of the prisoner's wounds, the camera even zooms in on the top of his head, which is criss-crossed with numerous red slashes. One of the man's rebel captors can be seen mocking the wounded prisoner as he struggles to remain conscious.

in the videos are often—though not exclusively—dark-skinned. It should be noted that these rumors have never been verified, despite their being widely reported as fact in the Western media. Many of the alleged "African mercenaries" were surely just regular soldiers in the Libyan army; others, simply immigrant workers with no connection to the conflict whatsoever.[2] In addition to soldiers and/or "mercenaries," the victims of the rebel atrocities appear also to have included police and members of other security forces or organizations associated with the *ancien régime*.

Especially in light of the "humanitarian" justification for foreign intervention in the Libyan war, the existence of the rebel atrocity videos is of obvious significance as such. This makes it all the more remarkable that they have gone almost entirely ignored by mainstream Western media and NGOs.

But given the nature of the atrocities in question—and indeed the very fact that they were filmed—the videos also provided some of the first clues of the rebels' ties to al-Qaeda and kindred Islamic terror groups. It has, after all, long been standard practice for Islamic terror groups to document their abuse of captives in grisly jihadist "snuff" videos. As touched upon in chapter 5, some jihadists point to Quranic sanction for their efforts to "cast dread into the hearts of the unbelievers," as Surah 8:12 puts it.[3] But, more fundamentally, terror as a tactic, regardless of its ideological underpinnings, can only be effective to the extent that it is publicized. This is why jihadists do not only commit atrocities; they let it be known that they commit atrocities. And this is why modern day jihadists film their atrocities and post the videos on the Internet.

The beheading and group execution videos released by Abu-Musab al-Zarqawi's al-Qaeda in Iraq provide some of the most grimly

---

2. See, for instance, the comments by Peter Bouckaert of Human Rights Watch in "Africans targeted as rebels hunt mercenaries," *The Age*, March 6, 2011.

3. For a discussion of this and related passages in the Quran, see Timothy R. Furnish, "Beheading in the Name of Islam," *Middle East Quarterly*, spring 2005.

famous examples. In light of the many connections between al-Qaeda in Iraq and the Libyan rebellion discussed above, it is undoubtedly no coincidence that the atrocities documented in the Libyan videos clearly recall the brutal methods of al-Zarqawi, including the jihadist form of retribution *par excellence*: beheading.

Perhaps the most well-known of the Libyan videos depicts the beheading of an alleged "mercenary" during the first days of the rebellion in February 2011. In a notable departure from the standard jihadist beheading videos, this beheading occurs in a public place in front of a large crowd. The place in question is none other than the symbolic cradle of the Libyan rebellion: the courthouse complex in Benghazi. Many members of the crowd can be seen filming the event on their cell phones. The victim has been suspended upside-down in front of an arched window on the ground floor of one of the courthouse buildings. Shouts of *"Allahu Akbar!"* ring out as a man with a long knife begins sawing at his neck.[4]

There is no doubt about the location. Indeed, in a report broadcast by CNN, Senator John McCain can be seen walking by the same building just two months later during a tour of the rebel capital.[5] Senator McCain, one of the earliest and most vocal American supporters of the rebellion, is accompanied by the late American ambassador to Libya, Chris Stevens. Stevens was, at the time, the US government's special envoy to the rebellion's "National Transitional Council." Even more chillingly, when then French President Nicolas Sarkozy and British Prime Minister David Cameron made their triumphant visit

---

4.   The Benghazi beheading video can be viewed at http://www.youtube.com/watch?v=vrAqcd5WgHY. It should be noted that after attention was first called to rebel atrocity videos in early spring 2011, YouTube made a regular practice of removing such videos or cancelling the accounts of users who post them. The author has copies in his possession of all the videos cited in this chapter.

5.   See John Rosenthal, "John McCain celebrated Libyan rebellion at site of rebels' public beheading, videos show," *The Daily Caller*, September 15, 2011.

to Benghazi in September 2011, they posed for photos in front of the very spot where the beheading had occurred.[6]

In early June 2011, the pro-Qaddafi website S.O.S. Libya posted a second beheading video, which, it claims, shows the execution by rebel forces of a member of the (pro-Qaddafi) Warfalla tribe. The victim is identified as one Hamza al-Gheit Fughi. The grisly video is shot as a close-up in the style of "classical" al-Qaeda beheading videos. As the man's head is completely severed from his body, cries of *"Allahu Akbar!"* ring out from members of the unseen assembly. Rhythmic muttering of *"Allahu Akbar!"* continues as the severed head is placed on the man's torso and then held up for the camera.[7]

Given the "classical" al-Qaeda style of the video, neither the location nor the perpetrators can be readily identified from the video itself. To this extent, the "Hamza al-Gheit Fughi" video must be treated with greater caution than the Benghazi beheading video. The soundtrack, however, would undoubtedly provide important clues for investigators attempting to establish the exact circumstances of the crime. But—like the numerous videos documenting easily verifiable "public" atrocities committed by the rebels—the "al-Gheit Fughi" video has simply been ignored by Western media and NGOs.

There is abundant evidence that rebel forces in fact made a regular practice of beheading their adversaries or slitting their throats. The latter amounts to a variant application of the injunction in Surahs 47:4 and 8:12 to "strike the necks of the unbelievers." Such evidence includes additional pictorial evidence of decapitated or partially decapitated corpses, the admissions of participants, and even the occasional passing reference in Western news reports. Thus, for example, a Reuters report from the scene of Muammar al-Qaddafi's capture outside Sirte

---

6. For the pictorial evidence, see John Rosenthal, "McCain is Not Alone: Sarko, Cameron Celebrate Libya Rebellion at Beheading Site," *Transatlantic Intelligencer*, September 24, 2011.

7. The "Hamza al-Gheit Fughi" beheading video can be viewed at http://libyasos. blogspot.com/2011/06/beheading-in-name-of-democracy-in-libya.html.

notes that one of the members of Qaddafi's personal guard had been decapitated, "his dreadlocked head lying beside his torso."[8] Amateur video of the scene shows that at least two other members of Qaddafi's party, including former Libyan Minister of Defense Abu Bakr Younis Jabr, appear to have had their throats slit.[9]

Other video clips from the early days of the rebellion provide clear proof of the summary execution of a group of up to 22 Libyan government soldiers. The soldiers' hands have been tied behind their backs and their eyes are bound. They have been shot in the back of the head, in the style of al-Zarqawi's al-Qaeda in Iraq. In one clip, men walking among the corpses can be heard repeating *"Allahu Akbar!"*

It is interesting to note that the pro-rebellion libyafeb17.com website posted footage of the dead soldiers as alleged evidence of an atrocity committed by Libyan government forces. On the account given by libyafeb17.com in its March 3, 2011 post, the men were supposed to be "soldiers executed by Gaddafi forces for refusing to shoot protesters."[10] Additional footage, however, clearly shows some of the same men alive and being interrogated by rebel captors. According to English sub-titles that have been added to some postings of the clip, their captors accuse them precisely of having fired on civilians.[11]

---

8. "Gaddafi caught like 'rat' in a drain, humiliated and shot," Reuters, October 21, 2011. For other examples of such passing references to rebel beheadings in the Western media, see "Libya Revolt as It Happened: Monday," BBC (website), March 7, 2011; "Dispatch from Libya: the courage of ordinary people standing up to Gaddafi," *The Guardian*, April 23, 2011; and "The headless corpse, the mass grave and worrying questions about Libya's rebel army," *The Telegraph*, July 20, 2011.

9. The video, which shows rebel forces gleefully desecrating the corpses, is viewable at http://www.youtube.com/watch?v=YudsOKSdnww.

10. The libyafeb17.com post can be consulted at http://www.libyafeb17.com/2011/03/graphic-footage-of-soldiers-executed-by-gaddafi-forces-for-refusing-to-shoot-protesters/. As of this writing, the video embedded in the post does not work.

11. For a more detailed discussion of the pertinent footage, see John Rosenthal, "Mounting Evidence of Rebel Atrocities in Libya," *Pajamas Media*, April 20, 2011. Poor quality versions of the two sequences cited here can be viewed at http://www.liveleak.com/view?i=d11_1301666809&c=1. Other copies of the relevant clips have been removed from YouTube, but are in the possession of the author.

As with the rebels' practice of beheading, there is in the meanwhile abundant evidence that the rebels also made a regular practice of summarily executing captured enemy soldiers by shots to the back of the head. This is in keeping with the take-no-prisoners—or, more exactly, keep-no-prisoners—philosophy of Abu Musab al-Zarqawi.

Some of this evidence has been re-cast by rebel spokespersons and Western media as evidence of atrocities committed by Qaddafi loyalist forces. But the circumstances obviously point to rebel responsibility. The bodies observed by Western journalists near Muammar al-Qaddafi's Bab al-Aziziya compound after the fall of Tripoli provide just one of many examples.[12] In contrast to the crude bindings used by the rebels in the early stages of the rebellion, photographs of the scene near Bab al-Aziziya show that the hands of some of the victims were tied behind their backs with state-of-the-art slender plastic handcuffs—presumably furnished by the rebels' Western allies.

Still other videos show live captives being subjected to exceptionally harsh treatment that clearly amounts to torture. One particularly harrowing clip, for example, shows two black African captives in army fatigues who have been tightly bound from head to foot. One of the men appears to be badly wounded. The other whimpers feebly as he attempts in vain to wriggle free from his bindings.[13]

Whereas the rebel atrocity videos have been passed over in silence by the mainstream Western media, in certain online forums, instead of provoking condemnation of the Libyan rebels, they have tended to provoke blanket condemnations of Muslims or Arabs as such. In this connection, it is worth pointing out that in several of the videos a "good Samaritan" can be seen and/or heard attempting to intervene to protect the victim or victims. This is the case, for instance, in the

---

12. See, for instance, Paul Schemm, "Bodies scattered next to Gaddafi compound," Associated Press, August 26, 2011.

13. The clip is available at http://www.liveleak.com/view?i=8eb_1299715342. The clearly pro-rebellion poster of the clip identifies the two victims as "mercenaries" who are "awaiting liquidation" in Misrata.

Benghazi beheading video. As a rule, the "good Samaritan" shouts "*Haram! Haram!*"—meaning that the rebels' treatment of their captives is forbidden by Islamic scripture.

CHAPTER 9

Abu Munthir's Plan

Although the Libyan rebellion was initially presented as a "protest movement" in the Western news media, it is perfectly clear from both video evidence and first-hand accounts that the "protests" were in fact extremely violent from the start. Before long, columns of armed "protestors"—as some Western media continued incongruously to call them—were marching toward Tripoli.

In virtually every city or town where unrest broke out, police stations and other government buildings and installations were attacked and set on fire. Such attacks were recorded in Benghazi, Derna, Tobruk, al-Bayda and al-Zawiya, among other places. In Derna, according to the testimony of pro-rebellion "activist" Amer Saad, Qaddafi loyalist forces were locked in the holding cells of a local police station and the building was set ablaze.[1]

---

1.   For Saad's account, see "Libya protests: massacres reported as Gaddafi imposes news blackout," *The Guardian*, February 18, 2011.

Little-known evidence cited in a British court case indicates that there was nothing spontaneous about the violence. The Libyan Islamic Fighting Group had elaborated a plan for destabilizing the Qaddafi regime that involved many of the tactics that were in fact employed at the outset of the Libyan rebellion in February 2011. A handwritten document setting out the plan was discovered by British police during an October 2005 raid of the home of a Libyan refugee in Birmingham. A CD discovered in the same residence contained a bomb-making manual, as well as what a British judge, in sentencing remarks, termed texts of a "general jihadist nature," including "lurid anti-western material."[2]

That the LIFG plan should have been discovered in the United Kingdom is not as surprising as it might appear at first glance. As touched upon above, numerous LIFG members are known to have taken refuge in the UK. As will be seen momentarily, the refugees even included some of the top leaders of the organization. Some of the LIFG members received formal asylum. Still others were granted leave to remain in the country even though their applications for asylum were rejected. They thus came to benefit from a sort of de facto asylum.

This was the case, for instance, of Ziyad al-Hashim, the LIFG "propagandist" with connections both to Abdul-Hakim Belhadj and to leading members of the Madrid trains plot. In deference to European human rights law, al-Hashim was granted leave to remain in the UK even though he was found, by virtue of his terror connections, to represent a "real and direct threat" to British national security.[3] The 2007 ruling would set a precedent, permitting, in effect, any and all LIFG members in the UK to avoid deportation, whether or not they had been formally granted asylum.[4]

---

2. Sentencing remarks of Mr. Justice Mackay. Quoted in Secretary of State for the Home Department v AV, April 30, 2009, paragraph 9.

3. Special Immigration Appeals Commission judgment of April 27, 2007, Appeal No: SC/42 and 50/2005 (paragraph 71).

4. See Secretary Of State For The Home Department–and–(1)AT (2)AW, March 20, 2009.

It is difficult to say just how many LIFG members settled in the UK. But it is clear that it is a substantial number and that by the middle of the last decade at the latest there was a bustling British LIFG "scene."

The United Nations list of al-Qaeda-linked persons and entities includes at least eight LIFG members who were living in the United Kingdom at the time of their listing.[5] A ninth UK-based Libyan with known links to the LIFG, Faraj Farj Hassan al-Saadi, was de-listed in September 2010 after reportedly being killed in a traffic accident.[6] Hassan al-Saadi—aka "Hamza Al Libi"—had been granted leave to remain in the UK in the same 2007 ruling from which Ziyad al-Hashim benefitted. He was granted leave to remain even though he had already been convicted by an Italian court of terrorism-related offenses—convicted, that is to say, in absentia, since British authorities failed to respond to an Italian extradition request in time for him to stand trial in person. Italian investigators suspect Hassan al-Saadi of having served as a European envoy for none other than Abu Musab al-Zarqawi and al-Qaeda in Iraq.[7]

Britain's own courts have, moreover, tried many cases brought by the Home Office against LIFG members residing in the country. The identities of the defendants are, however, almost invariably pro-

---

5.   As is typical of the UN list, the listings include many different aliases and alternate transliterations. But per the primary names given in the listings, the eight LIFG members are Abd Al-Rahman Al-Faqih, Ghuma Abd'rabbah, Abdulbaqi Mohammed Khaled, Tahir Nasuf, Mohammed Benhammedi, Abdulbasit Abdulrahim, Maftah Mohamed Elmabruk, and Abdelrazag Elsharif Elosta.

6.   Oddly enough, the September 9, 2010 UN press release announcing Hassan al Saadi's de-listing refers to a review of the listing concluded the prior January and it makes no mention of his reported death merely three weeks earlier. Hassan al Saadi has admitted to living with LIFG members in Peshawar for "nearly a year" until the end of 1999, but he claims that he was merely there to study and succeeded in learning "the whole of the Koran" during that time. See Secretary Of State For The Home Department—and—Faraj Faraj Hassan Al Saadi, December 21, 2009 (paragraph 11).

7.   See "Lite Milano-Londra sull' uomo di Zarkawi," *Corriere della Sera*, October 15, 2005. In the 2007 immigration court ruling, Hassan al-Saadi is merely identified as "AS."

tected—even when they have been convicted of terrorism-related offenses under Britain's own laws!

Thus, in a 2009 British court ruling, the Birmingham-based possessor of the LIFG plan to topple Qaddafi is identified merely by the initials "AV." The ruling notes that AV was a member of the LIFG's governing Shura Council and that his name was added to the United Nations list of al-Qaeda linked individuals and entities on February 7, 2006.[8]

These and other biographical details make clear that "AV" is none other than Abd Al-Rahman al-Faqih: the LIFG Shura Council member whom we met in chapter 5 attending strategy meetings in Turkey and who would go on to be convicted in absentia by a Moroccan court of complicity in the May 2003 Casablanca suicide bombings. The Moroccan conviction is mentioned in both the British ruling and the UN summary of the reasons for al-Faqih's inclusion on the UN terror list. Al-Faqih was granted asylum in the UK in September 2004, i.e. barely one year after the Casablanca bombings.[9] He had arrived in the country two years earlier in September 2002.

The UN summary of reasons notes, furthermore, that al-Faqih—like Faraj Farj Hassan al-Saadi—is "assessed to have had connections to the terrorist network in Iraq which was led by Abu Musab al-Zarqawi."[10] Indeed, in British court proceedings, al-Faqih tacitly admitted his links to al-Zarqawi's al-Qaeda in Iraq, claiming that he had sent a message to the captors of Kenneth Bigley in an effort to

---

8. See Secretary of State for the Home Department v AV, April 30, 2009. The ruling mistakenly identifies the relevant UN Security Council Committee as the "1263 Committee." The correct designation is the 1267 Committee.

9. Moreover, al-Faqih is not the only LIFG member living in the UK who has been convicted of involvement in the Casablanca bombings. According to the 2007 al-Hashim/Hassan al-Saadi immigration ruling, there is a second one, although the name is not given. See Special Immigration Appeals Commission judgment of April 27, 2007, Appeal No: SC/42 and 50/2005 (paragraph 63).

10. See UN Security Council 1267 Committee, Narrative Summary of Reasons for Listing: Abd Al-Rahman Al-Faqih.

persuade the latter to spare Bigley's life.[11] Bigley, a British civil engineer, was beheaded by al-Zarqawi's group in October 2004.

According to al-Faqih's statements, the author of the plan discovered in his possession appears to have been LIFG chief ideologue Abu al-Munthir al-Saadi. Al-Faqih says that he received the original draft of the document from al-Munthir after his arrival in the United Kingdom in late 2002.[12]

As it so happens, a certain Abu Munthir has been cited in other British court proceedings as an al-Qaeda operative who encouraged young Muslims in Great Britain to conduct terror attacks at home following the invasion of Afghanistan. Several of the young Britons had travelled to Pakistan in early 2003, in order to join the jihad against the American invaders and their coalition allies. There they met up with Salahuddin Amin, a slightly older compatriot with a direct line to the upper echelons of the al-Qaeda hierarchy: namely, by virtue of his association with the said Abu Munthir. According to Amin, after consultation with the al-Qaeda leadership, Abu Munthir rebuffed the young Britons' desire to join the frontlines of jihad in Afghanistan. "If they really want to do something," Abu Munthir told him, "then go back [to the UK] and you can do something there."[13]

If Abu Munthir's advice sounds strangely familiar, that is because it is precisely the strategy upon which the leadership of the LIFG had agreed with other North African al-Qaeda affiliates in their 2002 Istanbul meeting. (See chapter 5.) Muslims did not have to travel to active war zones in Muslim countries in order to participate in jihad; rather, they could undertake operations in their places of residence, notably, in the West. The idea was, in effect, to bring the frontlines to the enemy.

---

11. Secretary of State for the Home Department v AV, paragraph 17.
12. Secretary of State for the Home Department v AV, paragraph 15.
13. Salahuddin Amin, answers to questioning by Metropolitan Police, Paddington Green Police Station, February 8, 2005.

The young Britons would take Abu Munthir's advice to heart, returning to the United Kingdom some months later and preparing to manufacture ammonium nitrate bombs to be used in a series of simultaneous strikes on local targets in what would come to be known as the "Fertilizer Plot." With a view to maximizing civilian casualties, the prospective targets included not only the British power grid, but also a popular nightclub and a shopping center.

Before returning home in August 2003, plot leader Omar Khyam is reported to have met personally with Abu Munthir in Pakistan's northwestern tribal areas, in order to receive further guidance. "At this time, [Khyam] didn't have any . . . specific targets," one witness has testified, "He just had general ideas. So, the plan was to go back and to discuss specific targets, how they would be carried out . . . everything like that with Abu Munthir."[14]

Even after the other plotters returned to the United Kingdom, Abu Munthir would continue to serve as the plot's guru via the intermediary of Salahuddin Amin, who remained in Pakistan. By February 2004, Khyam had already acquired 650 kilograms of ammonium nitrate. But he was not sure how to mix the material with other chemicals in order to make explosives. Thus, he contacted Amin, who in turn contacted Abu Munthir, who provided the required bomb-making specifications.[15]

The e-mail exchange between Khyam and Amin was reportedly intercepted by the US National Security Agency and the information then passed on to British authorities. Shortly thereafter, in March, British police intervened to break up the plot and arrest the UK-based conspirators. But the guiding idea of Abu Munthir would live on

---

14. Testimony of Junaid Babar. Cited in Her Majesty The Queen–against–Moham-mad Momin Khawaja, Ontario Superior Court Of Justice, October 29, 2008, paragraph 21.

15. Crown Opening Statement, Regina v. Omar Khyam, Anthony Garcia, Nabeel Hussain, Jawad Akbar, Waheed Mahmood, Shujah-Ud-Din Mahmood, and Salahuddin Amin, March 21, 2006, paragraph 178.

and be brought to fruition one year later in the July 7, 2005 London transport bombings.

Two of the four suicide bombers — Shehzad Tanweer and plot leader Mohammed Siddique Khan—had ties to the leader of the Fertilizer Plot, Omar Khyam. Surveillance of Khyam by British domestic intelligence reveals that in the weeks leading up to his arrest, Khyam met no less than four times with Tanweer and Khan. Some of their conversations were recorded. The discussions revolved around the plans of Tanweer and Khan to join a jihadist camp in the tribal areas of Pakistan. The tenor of the conversations makes clear that Khyam served, in effect, as the handler of the two future bombers on behalf of the jihadist networks that were to host them, as well indeed as their mentor in the ways of global jihad.[16] Tanweer and Khan would go on to make such a trip to Pakistan later in the year.

Moreover, it is known that Khan, the "7/7" plot leader, already attended a terror training camp with Khyam in Pakistan in summer 2003. Khyam helped to set up the camp in Malakand, on the edge of the tribal areas and not far from the Afghan border. It was at this time that Khyam met with Abu Munthir, in order to discuss plans for terror attacks in the United Kingdom. According to the testimony of one of Khyam's associates, Khyam was hoping, among other things, to mount a suicide attack and he had been attempting to recruit a participant at the Malakand camp to this end.[17]

Salahuddin Amin is supposed to have first met Abu Munthir sometime in 1999 or 2000 at a mosque in Luton, not far from London. This fact would appear to rule out that the Abu Munthir of the Fertilizer Plot is *the* Abu Munthir: the famous "Sheikh of the Arabs

---

16. See "MI5 transcript of bomber's conversation," Channel 4 News (UK), May 1, 2007; and "Real Spooks," *Panorama*, BBC1, April 30, 2007.

17. Testimony of Junaid Babar. Cited in Her Majesty The Queen–against–Mohammad Momin Khawaja, Ontario Superior Court Of Justice, October 29, 2008, paragraph 21.

in Afghanistan," as Taliban leader Mullah Omar dubbed the LIFG's supreme ideological authority.

Or would it? A complaint filed by Hong Kong-based lawyers for Sami "Abu al-Munthir" al-Saadi contains an extraordinary revelation. Abd Al-Rahman al-Faqih is not the highest-ranking member of the LIFG to have lived in the United Kingdom. That honor belongs rather to none other Abu al-Munthir al-Saadi. According to the representations of his lawyers, al-Saadi arrived in the United Kingdom in 1993 and was granted indefinite leave to remain one year later.[18]

There is strong reason to believe that the "Abu Munthir" of the Fertilizer Plot is none other than the LIFG's Abu al-Munthir al-Saadi, and there is equally strong reason to believe that American and British authorities believed this when Abu al-Munthir was detained and "rendered" to Libya in early March, 2004.[19] Chronology also suggests this conclusion. Abu Munthir was detained just weeks after the interception of the e-mail exchange between Khyam and Amin, which cited his bomb-making guidance, and merely two weeks before Khyam and several co-conspirators were arrested in the UK.

The apparent identity of the al-Qaeda guru of the British Muslim plotters and the LIFG's Abu al-Munthir is all the more significant in light of additional testimony from Salahuddin Amin. According to Amin, "his" Abu Munthir did not only encourage young Britons to conduct terror attacks at home, he was also involved in efforts to purchase a "radioisotope bomb," i.e. a "dirty" nuclear weapon.[20]

---

18. Ho, Tse Wai & Partners, "Claim on behalf of Mr Sami Al-Saadi against HK-SARG," June 12, 2012.

19. It is notable that the British daily *The Guardian*, which has painted al-Munthir/al-Saadi as a "victim" of joint American and British wrongdoing, also comes to this conclusion. See "Libyan papers show UK worked with Gaddafi in rendition operation," *The Guardian*, September 4, 2011. The *Guardian* report even suggests, without quite saying it, that Salahuddin Amin identified al-Munthir from a photograph.

20. Crown Opening Statement, Regina v. Omar Khyam, Anthony Garcia, Nabeel Hussain, Jawad Akbar, Waheed Mahmood, Shujah-Ud-Din Mahmood, and Salahuddin Amin, March 21, 2006, paragraph 173. According to Amin, Abu Munthir asked him to contact a certain "Abu Annis" who was attempting to purchase the bomb. In statements provided to Human Rights Watch, the name is transliterated rather as "Abu Anas." See

In the early years of the new millennium, after being chased from Afghanistan, Abu Munthir, Belhadj and the LIFG appear to have been operating on multiple fronts: making major contributions to the global conspiratorial jihad against the "far enemy," the United States and its closest allies, while still planning for the great day when they would be able to bring about the demise of their much-hated "near enemy," Muammar al-Qaddafi and his "apostate" regime in Libya. According to the above-cited 2009 British court ruling, al-Munthir's plan for toppling Qaddafi included:

> . . . a call for mujahedin to train in the handling of weapons and the preparation of explosives and for them to inflict destruction and damage on "the headquarters of the revolutionary committees, the centres of the intelligence and the places of the revolutionaries and corrupters."[21]

The "revolutionaries" targeted by al-Munthir's plan were, in effect, any and all supporters of Muammar al-Qaddafi's so-called al-Fateh Revolution. The "revolutionary committees" were a permanent feature of Libyan society under Qaddafi, a form of institutionalization of the al-Fateh Revolution.

The plan called, furthermore, for a "martyrdom operation"—in other words, a suicide bombing—against "a big and important target such as the tyrant Qaddaffi, other prominent tyrants or centres of intelligence service."[22] As it so happens, a "martyrdom operation"

Cruel Britannia (Human Rights Watch, 2009), p. 23. (It should be noted that in his statements to Human Rights Watch, Amin denies knowing the person in question.) The contact is perhaps Abu Anas al-Libi: yet another high-level al-Qaeda operative and LIFG member to have taken refuge in the United Kingdom. Al-Libi, aka Nazih Abdul Hamed Al-Raghie, is under indictment in the US for his alleged role in the 1998 US embassy bombings in Tanzania and Kenya. He went into hiding prior to a British police raid on his home in Manchester in May 2000, and he appears to have fled the country around this time.

21. Secretary of State for the Home Department v AV, paragraph 15.
22. Secretary of State for the Home Department v AV, paragraph 8.

against military barracks in Benghazi on February 20, 2011 is reported to have played a key role in the success of the Libyan rebellion. The bomber is supposed to have loaded a car with explosives and blown open the gates to the barracks.

The very fact that the rebels would employ the signature method of al-Qaeda—the suicide bombing—is itself, of course, further evidence of their jihadist inspiration. Highly similar "martyrdom operations," involving vehicles packed with explosives, have been used against American military installations in Afghanistan.[23] The fact that the alleged Benghazi bomber has been hailed as a hero in Western news reports represents just one of the ways in which the Libya conflict resulted in what might be described as the "mainstreaming" of jihad.[24]

On the basis of his possession of the LIFG plan, Abd Al-Rahman al-Faqih was found guilty by a British court of possessing a document conducive to the commission or preparation of acts of terrorism in violation of the 2000 UK Terrorism Act. A February 2007 ruling upholding the conviction notes bluntly:

> . . . the legislation does not exempt, nor make an exception, nor create a defence for, nor exculpate what some would describe as terrorism in a just cause. Such a concept is foreign to the Act. Terrorism is terrorism, whatever the motives of the perpetrators.[25]

This is to say that in conjunction with American, French and other NATO forces, British forces intervened in Libya in support of

---

23. For the details of such an attack on an American guard post in Afghanistan's Khost province, see John Rosenthal, "Germany's Taliban Trail: From Murat Kurnaz to Cüneyt Ciftci" *World Politics Review*, May 14, 2008.

24. For celebrations of the Benghazi bomber in the Western media, see "The Situation Room" (online transcript), CNN, March 24, 2011; and "Dispatch from Libya: the courage of ordinary people standing up to Gaddafi," *The Guardian*, April 23, 2011.

25. R[egina] v F, February 16, 2007, paragraph 27. In the original ruling against him, al-Faqih was identified merely by the initial "F."

a rebellion whose methods the British courts had themselves found to constitute terrorism. This fact is all the more remarkable in light of the abundance of available evidence that the LIFG was equally committed to using the same methods against Western targets, including in the United Kingdom itself.

It is difficult to know more complete details of Abu al-Munthir's plan, because the British courts have made it difficult. The courts' insistence on protecting the identities of terror suspects—and even indeed convicted terrorists!—has created a bizarre catch-22, whereby court employees plead inability to handle requests for information on account of not having the defendants' full names! But even when the names are inferred and provided, the results are not necessarily any better. Repeated requests by the present author for transcripts in the case of Abd Al-Rahman al-Faqih have gone unfulfilled. According to court reporters, the corresponding tapes *might* have been destroyed. To this day, court reporters have provided no confirmation of whether they have been destroyed or any other explanation for their inability to fulfill the transcript request.

But one thing appears certain: Abu al-Munthir and his co-conspirators could not have imagined that their dreams of toppling Qaddafi would come to be realized with the help of the very Western powers against which they spent much of the last decade fighting and plotting. The fact of the matter is that Abu al-Munthir's plan was doomed to failure. The LIFG could have created death and destruction, just as it had created death and destruction before in Libya and just as, in conjunction with al-Qaeda and other al-Qaeda affiliated terror organizations, it had created death and destruction in the West. But the eastern Libyan uprising would have surely been put down by Libyan government forces in a matter of days had it not been for NATO bombing.

The exploits of the al-Qaeda-linked heroes of the Libyan revolution whom we have met above—rebel commanders like Abdul-Hakim al-Hasadi, Abdul-Hakim Belhadj and Wisam bin Hamid—are similarly illusory. It was NATO bombing that permitted al-Hasadi's forces to overrun Ajdabiya; and it was NATO bombing that permitted Belhadj's forces to walk in and take control of Tripoli; just as it was NATO bombing that permitted bin Hamid to win the Battle of Sirte and that ultimately drove Muammar al-Qaddafi into the hands of his tormentors and killers on the outskirts of the city. The "men of the Caliphate" did not conquer Libya, after all. It was rather NATO and the "infidel" governments of Paris, London and Washington that conquered Libya for them.

ACKNOWLEDGMENTS

This book would never have been written, much less published, were it not for Andrew McCarthy. I would like to thank Andy for the interest he took in the project and his invaluable help in finding an appropriate outlet for it.

Like Andy, Diana West was one of the very few American political commentators who refused to shield their eyes from the evidence of the Libyan rebellion's radical Islamic roots. Many thanks to Diana for her interest, encouragement and counsel during the course of the project's realization.

Maureen Millington-Brodie's translations from Arabic were indispensable to the completion of this book. I would like to thank Maureen for her contributions, not only for the translations themselves, but also for her keen observations and her patient didactic responses to my follow-up queries.

Thanks to Heather Ohle and Katherine Wong of Encounter for their work in preparing the manuscript for publication (and to Heather too for "getting" my idea for the book cover). Thanks too to Lauren Miklos and Sam Schneider of Encounter for their help.

Finally, special thanks to K and A, for bringing light into a period devoted to a very grim subject.

INDEX

CPSIA information can be obtained
at www.ICGtesting.com
Printed in the USA
JSHW022219071122
32755JS00001B/108